LIFTED

ADVENTURES IN RIDESHARING

JARED QUAN

COPYRIGHTS

Copyright © 2022 Jared Quan
Cover Design by Ahnasariah Larsen
Cover Images from Pixabay.com

ISBN (print): 979-8-218-06957-5

Distributed by Big World Network.
1st Edition 2022.
Interior Design by Ahnasariah Larsen

OTHER TITLES BY JARED QUAN

Ezekiel's Gun

Changing Wax

Shattered Worlds

TABLE OF CONTENTS

To the hard-working people who rely on side gigs just to keep from drowning. You have put in the work and deserve so much more.

And to the souls who keep the gas station bathroom clean. It's a thankless job that made driving rideshare bearable. You are my hero.

JARED QUAN

LIFTED

ADVENTURES IN RIDESHARING

Introduction

I started driving rideshare for the money: my son needed a heart transplant, and we needed the extra income. It wasn't long before driving strangers became a passion. Not long after that, an addiction. I craved the truly unpredictable nature of the next call. I realized that I could be picking up anyone—a famous person, a politician, a CEO, someone with a remarkable story—and I could be headed anywhere. As the rides became adventures, I started writing them down.

In three years and three months, I completed 1,947 rides. I also finished with a five-star rating, which is both true and not. Drivers out there will tell you that there are people who never give five stars no matter what you do. My lifetime average rating is 4.94. The app tells passengers that I'm an even 5.0.

I pondered a great deal about how to start a book documenting some of the most improbable events as a Rideshare Driver. I am truly excited to share bizarre tales of college students on Halloween, billionaires dressed as bums, the inebriated, the tumultuous, possibly the Russian mafia, and much more.

Where it all Began

Our second oldest son, Jared Jackson Quan, was named after me (Jared) and my father (Jackson). Jack was born with a rare version of Hypoplastic Left Heart Syndrome (HLHS). He essentially only had two chambers in his heart, as opposed to the normal four. The combination of variants was so out of the ordinary that the most experienced heart surgeon of more than twenty years had not seen the like before.

My wife and I had been home with our new baby for less than twenty-four hours when the doctors laid out our options. In a best-case scenario, Jack would undergo several surgeries and procedures to keep him alive until a transplant opened up. He had a ten-percent chance of making it that far. We were shellshocked. Our other options were to move to San Diego or Denver and put Jack on an infant transplant list, or do nothing at all and let him expire.

In Jack's situation, there were three major open-heart surgeries he would endure. They gave him that high of a chance partly because his surgeon, Dr. John Hawkins, was one of the top pediatric cardiovascular surgeons in the nation. During his twenty years, he had done these surgeries countless times.

Each time we took him to Primary Children's Medical Center, we braced ourselves with that ten percent chance in mind. The Norwood (2 months old), the Bidirectional Glenn (18 months), the Fontan (4 years old), and numerous minor procedures in between.

During this time Jack gained the nickname "Smiling Jack" because of his infectious positive attitude. Everyone, from Dr. Hawkins to the janitors we saw all the time at Primary Children's, was nothing short of brilliant. Everyone was friendly and caring, which always contributed to the hope and healing.

This was all complicated by the discovery that he was autistic, and potentially had brain damage from insufficient oxygen during his early years of development. We sought out official testing for a diagnosis when it was clear that there were struggles in school.

In 2017, his oxygen saturation dropped too low without constant O2 assistance, and the pressures in his body reached a concerning level. The heart team at Primary Children's moved Jack to the transplant team. The new team ran a battery of additional tests before adding him to the transplant list. There are four different statuses one can be listed under:

Status 1a—A patient's heart is failing; they are bound to a medical facility and can't leave without a new heart.

Status 1b—A patient's heart is starting to fail, to the point that they are in and out of medical facilities often.

Status 2—A patient's heart is starting to deteriorate at a rate that they will need a new heart, but are stable enough to spend more time at home.

Status 7—This is a temporary suspension of being active on the list. You don't lose your place, but you can't be called up to get a new heart.

Jack was assigned to Status 2 and remained there for just under three years.

Fifteen days before the third anniversary of his listing, we got the call on a December Sunday morning in 2020. This was the last thing we would expect, partly because Jack had been on the list for a long time as a lower priority status, and because the world was in the middle of the COVID-19 pandemic outbreak.

We got to the hospital and prepared for a long wait. Jack's surgery had an estimated completion time of 14 hours. This was due to the scar tissue from previous surgeries, and the prep his body needed to work correctly with a fully functional heart.

We were educated early on as to how the transplant system works. There are variables that must be met to ensure a high chance of success in a transplant patient. When a donor has been identified, they run a series of tests and evaluate the quality of the organ. Then the Organ Procurement and Transportation Network goes to work to get the organ to the right patient.

They screen out candidates that are incompatible due to blood type, height, weight, age, and other medical factors. Then they narrow it down by geographic location. Each donated organ has its own limited window of viability. Hearts have the shortest window of time they are good. The transplant must be completed within 4–6 hours of being removed from the donor. From there, the list narrows one last time by organ size.

With all these factors in mind, we had an idea of the profile of our donor. The individual that had paid the ultimate sacrifice, and then elected to selflessly save at least eight people. The candidate was a smaller person, most likely a female, between the ages of sixteen and twenty-five. They did not pass away from a traumatic situation like a car accident; they did not suffer from any major illness. This means the death was likely sudden and unexpected.

We are filled with gratitude beyond explanation when we think about the young woman who may have been married, had a partner, had children, been in college, or working to make ends meet. We are haunted by the thought that the day before we got the call, they were alive and well. Their whole future was ahead of them. Young as they were, the potential was staggering. And then it was taken from them, tragically, on short notice. I feel for the family. I feel for them even more when I think that in the middle of a global pandemic, very few of them would have been able to gather to celebrate that bright star which had gone out too soon.

As Jack recovered quickly from the transplant, our thoughts were also with the family of Dr. John Hawkins, who had passed away in 2009. He had saved countless lives, and didn't get to see Jack beat the ten percent odds given at birth.

Jack's recovery was remarkable. Just two weeks after the transplant, he was cleared.

However, at that point, there was another complication. While Jack was in the hospital, the rest of the family came down with COVID-19. Though my wife spent a brief stint in the hospital on Christmas day, the family recovered with lingering effects. Jack returned home with his brand-new heart in January 2021, and we celebrated Christmas when he came home.

That celebration was extra special thanks to the brilliant support of family, friends, and acquaintances that had been following our family's journey. We extend a special place in our hearts for those individuals who made all the difference in a difficult and crazy time.

~*~

You might be asking at what point my son's heart put me in a car driving rideshare. The answer: 2017, when he was put on the transplant list.

It was surrealistic. We'd known, since his birth, that at some point he'd need a transplant—but the sudden reality of it happening took us by surprise. My wife Lisa and I attended mandatory classes to understand everything from medication to expenses to paperwork to statistics to how the transplant team operates. It was after bootcamp that we reviewed our finances and realized we wouldn't make it. The cost of medications and hospital visits, the tests, the surgery itself: financially, we were sunk.

I decided to approach my employer to see what could be done. I had served the company faithfully for many years. I had taken on big projects, and I was redefining what was possible in my role. Both my supervisor and my boss bandied compliments like, 'No one can do what you do,' and 'you're invaluable.' So I thought, reasonably, that I could be considered for a promotion, or a raise, or at least a career path that would map with my future expenses.

Instead, I was handed a copy of Dave Ramsey's book, *The Total Money Makeover*. They told me the company could not envision me in a different role. It wasn't the feedback or direction I was hoping for, but the book helped.

Lisa and I looked elsewhere for funds. We discovered two parttime jobs flexible enough to not intrude on my fulltime work. One was working security for a company that contracts with Real Salt Lake, the Depot, the Eccles Theater, and other individual projects as needed. *That* job warrants its own book of stories, much like this one.

The other parttime opening was rideshare.

The nice part of driving rideshare was the lack of a set schedule. I could do it whenever I was available, in whatever scraps of time I had open in a day. As soon as I clocked out of my day job, I could log into ridesharing. The other attractant was an offered bonus of $2,000 if you completed 100 rides within the first 30 days.

Two grand was enough to pay for one of Jack's immunosuppressants for a single month. It was also the typical bill after insurance for something like a biopsy, which happened multiple times a year. It was crazy to learn that an uninsured transplant patient would cost close to $10,000 a month in just medications, for half a year after the surgery. Then you add the required follow-up appointments, prescription changes, and tests, and the cost quickly becomes astronomical.

Thankfully, we had insurance. Our maximum out-of-pocket cost was $7,500 for the family, so that was the goal. Build up enough savings to cover the out-of-pocket, and then maintain enough surplus to cover a year.

There were two rideshare companies available. I initially signed up with both, then quickly realized it was a mistake. I could realistically hit the bonus with only one of them. So I trudged through company reviews, thought it through, and chose. I had no idea that I would be joining over 6,000 registered rideshare drivers in Salt Lake County alone. Funny enough, two of the drivers were retired heart surgeons. They gave rides in their very expensive vehicles for the express purpose of talking to people.

The job requirements were simple enough: have a newer four-door vehicle, a valid driver's license, and pass a background check. My vehicle, a 2015 Dodge Journey, counted as a plus vehicle. This meant I could answer calls for both everyday passengers and larger groups of five. Sometimes it meant four people and a ton of luggage. It generated rides that were longer and paid better. And since it had all-wheel drive and brand-new tires, we felt it was a safe vehicle to take into the line of work.

I wasn't sure if I was going to enjoy or hate the experience. Like many authors, I was an introvert. On the bright side, I had already been training—unintentionally. I volunteered for several local organizations. This often put me in front of people, and pushed me to expand my interpersonal skillset. It even landed me special guest spots at writing conferences and the Salt Lake FanX. Need has a way of moving people out of their comfort zone.

The upside to driving for rideshare companies was that the longer I did it, the better I was, the more people I met, and the more I got to know Utah. It was funny: after living in Utah for fifteen years, I thought I knew and understood the roads. Rideshare showed me new routes, hidden corners, and new insights into the city layouts. This is a book about the people I met, but the stories here barely scratch the surface of what I learned.

The downside to rideshare was the slog. It was staying out later than I expected, finding the right gas station, sometimes long wait times, disappointing results, the wear and tear of extra miles on the car. There were many instances where I needed just one more ride to hit a bonus and missed it. Or there was one, but it took me 45 minutes further away from home. There is always a gas station out there, somewhere, that is 10 to 20 cents cheaper per gallon than even Sam's Club or Costco. But finding it, and then getting to it at the right time, could be a challenge. Sometimes there were too many rideshare drivers on the roads, or too few customers in the area, or I was out of range of the crowd. Some days were just slow.

I must warn people also that not every driving day was lucrative. Some days you don't get more than a single ride, which leaves you in the negative against the gas consumed.

The absolute worst part is vehicular wear. I was never in an accident and no one threw up in my car, but sweaty alcohol and overapplied aromatics are not smells you can exorcise. We drove our kids to school and went on family trips in that vehicle. You never forget your kids' reactions to those smells.

Then there is the dreaded check engine light, because deep in your gut you know a vehicle repair will wipe you out. For us, it was the transmission. A $2,000 gut punch to your savings sets you back a great deal.

We never hit our financial goals before the pandemic put an end to driving rideshare. Transplant patients are put on immunosuppressants to prevent their bodies from rejecting the new organ; the risk to Jack wasn't worth it.

We did make through, and we enjoyed some crazy jobs. I hope to provide you with some entertainment from the chaos. For those keeping score, during that time I: had a fulltime day job; worked security for CSC; was a teacher on the Utah Artist Teaching Roster for the Utah Arts Council, now the Utah Department of Arts and Museums; taught at several conferences, including FanX Salt Lake City; and volunteered on the West Jordan Arts Council, the Eagle Mountain Arts Alliance, the League of Utah Writers Presidency, TEDxSaltLakeCity, and the Storymakers Board. Rideshare filled the gaps between meetings and events.

From then to now

Everyone I drive, and everyone I talk to about rideshare, asks me similar questions: What is it like? Do I enjoy it? Who is the worst passenger I have had? What is the coolest story I have?

I have answered these questions hundreds of times. Every day that I climbed into my vehicle to drive to work or to volunteer, I could still hear and smell the passengers. The surfaces of the vehicle absorbed bits of essential oils, expensive fragrances, food, smoke, alcohol, sometimes an unpleasant stench of unknown origin. As air circulated, I would imagine the passengers with such clarity: talking, laughing, sleeping, and sometimes crying.

With every story told, another was demanded: like an unsatisfied itch, the audience always wanted more. I decided to take my own advice and assemble a book. This book, specifically. It contains stories of both good and bad passengers, personal reflections, poems written between rides. These are all true stories. I have, however, changed names and locations to protect the identities of those involved.

The Start of the Rideshare Day

It feels a bit like Doctor Who. My Dodge Journey is the Tardis: it's bigger on the inside than you'd expect, seating seven total. And just as the Doctor flits between people and planets, ridesharing slides you from adventure to adventure, passenger to passenger, place to person to place.

The day begins when I leave my daytime workplace, opening the door to the silver Dodge Journey and slipping behind the steering wheel. I look back at the office building through the windshield; it feels like nodding goodbye to an old friend. Then it's a sigh to settle myself after a full shift, a push of the start button for the ignition, a swipe across my phone to open the rideshare app as my vehicle thrums alive.

As my hands rise to the wheel, I feel like Jason Statham in *The Transporter,* ready to take on the next assignment. Like I'm waiting in a high-precision vehicle to take to the road. My thoughts turn to driving: to navigating the city, to the unpredictable drivers with whom I will share the road.

My eyes drop to my phone as it begins to buzz. The first rideshare passenger is now expecting me. According to the map, they are ten minutes away. I nod encouragement to myself in the rearview mirror, and shift into gear.

At that moment, a cocktail of emotion hits me. Adrenaline, excitement, nervousness. Anxiety. I am an introvert. I am tired after a full day in the office. I am embarking in a line of work that is about strangers.

How I Rideshare as a Driver

Being a rideshare driver is opening yourself up to amazing experiences, if you let it. There are some things you can do to increase your chances of having extraordinary stories. I approach driving people the same way I play a video game. Every ride/video game is a story to be unlocked. The challenge's parameters include factors like the length of ride, the number of people, their sobriety, and how introverted or extroverted they lean. Sometimes I am very successful. Sometimes I fail pretty hard.

This is how I approach each ride.

First Impressions

For me, the first impression is vital to making a connection with the passenger/s. On days I am driving rideshare I carefully choose what clothing I am going to wear. When I first started, I wore a suit and tie because that is what I wore to the office, and I started driving immediately after work. I had no idea how this would impact my experiences.

During one ride, a psychology major from the University of Utah explained to me that dressing in a suit and tie takes advantage of "person perception." Our cognitive processes are involved in categorizing people. It is the same mechanism that helps us shortcut the process of deciding who to trust.

For me, the first impression is vital to making a connection with the passenger/s. On days I am driving rideshare I carefully choose what clothing I am going to wear. When I first started, I wore a suit and tie because that is what I wore to the office, and I started driving immediately after work. I had no idea how this would impact my experiences.

A passenger begins processing details, mostly subconsciously, based on past experience before they even enter the vehicle. Everything is processed, from the profile picture to the rating to the vehicle type. Even the vehicle's color influences the passenger's perception.

The psychology major compared it to what Sherlock Holmes does in the newest iterations. We essentially do the same thing in a few seconds. We judge if someone is trustworthy, high status, smart, successful, friendly, etc; we make assumptions and judgments on lifestyle, activities, age, and limitations. These are based on the clothes, hairstyle, facial features, posture, tattoos, and various other minute details. Though we don't consciously catalogue these details, we subconsciously associate them with the memory of that person moving forward. Once we have this impression locked in, it becomes difficult for someone to change it. This is where some biases and stereotypes live.

When the psychologist and I arrived at their destination, we sat and continued the conversation. I was curious about how to augment or change the snapshot judgments we make. Also, how do we escape the preconceived biases or stereotypes that we have built? I wanted to ensure that I was giving everyone a fair chance. The conversation went on for an additional fifteen minutes at least.

What it boiled down to is a need for willingness, a conscious effort, for communication and application. Force yourself to think about what is happening when you see someone, and when possible, have a conversation with the person. This creates an experience that future snapshots will be connected to. The idea is to create a very large sample size of experiences for your subconscious to utilize.

I can't tell you of all the rides where I picked up someone who was in a dark mood, and the conversation during the drive left them in a positive place. That human interaction is priceless.

Part of the problem is that often time we rely on the experiences of others, or things we see or hear on the news, to substitute for an in-person interaction. It can be difficult to get out and create new experiences, especially when something like a global pandemic is happening. But it is possible. I personally recommend volunteering in the community. Often it will take you out of your comfort zone, and into spaces where you work with a great diversity of people and experience.

I can work on controlling my snapshot judgments. I can't control how others snapshot judge me, but I can influence it. The first step: wear something nice.

If you're out and about, I don't actually recommend a suit. They're uncomfortable. They're hot. They itch. And they're more formal than most occasions warrant. But *do* wear something nice. Avoid jeans and a t-shirt (unless what you're doing is manual labor), and go for something with high visibility. I like to interchange a fedora, a bowler hat, and a classic flat driver's hat.

A Dickens Twist

A little past my first full year driving rideshare, there was a ride that I summarize as a Dicken's Twist. I considered myself a seasoned veteran at that point. I had met a lot of people, heard a lot of stories, covered a lot of roads. On that particular Saturday, I was summoned to the airport from downtown. While not precisely common, it was known to happen every now and then.

The morning was overcast and threatening to rain. Mostly the clouds had managed to work up a spit and gusty winds. This was frustrating weather to work in, because it made the dust and the dirt of Salt Lake stick to your car. Normally clean and well-maintained vehicles were left looking like they'd never seen a wash. I ran mine through at least once a day, sometimes twice; I had a subscription to the local chain of carwashes. They're almost as common as McDonalds now.

As I approached the airport, there was a rare break in the clouds. The Salt Lake airport was in the middle of renovations and under heavy construction. The designated pickup and drop-off zones made sense, thankfully, but required a very slow approach. I remember the radio playing "Shotgun" by George Ezra. As I neared the Delta terminal, I hit the button on the rideshare app to let my passenger know I was there. Then I stopped the car, got out, and opened the trunk in anticipation of their luggage. This was a routine I had completed over a hundred times.

No one seemed to be approaching, but the app had confirmed that they were ready at the pickup zone. This was normal. Often, the passenger would make the rideshare request as they were exiting the plane, and still had to walk the mile or so to the pickup zone. One of the airport police began to watch me with concern. I knew that if my pickup didn't emerge shortly, my five-minute window would be closed, and I would have to circle the entire airport and try again. This would typically create a very irritated passenger or a canceled ride.

I let out a sigh of relief when a well-dressed man with high-end suitcases started walking my way. A big smile crossed my face as I took a step toward them.

"Dave?" I asked. A disappointing shake of the head left me embarrassed and concerned. At this point, the airport police officer started to slowly walk in my direction. Rumors of drivers being ticketed for abusing the pickup and drop-off began to flood my mind. The few rays of sunshine that would reach the floor of the Salt Lake Valley that day were choked by the returning storm clouds. A gust of wind tried to pull the fedora from my head and nearly toppled the officer. Large drops of rain began to smash into the pavement.

"Sir!" The officer called.

I pointed to myself as if there were another driver next to me. It reminded me of school dances I would go to as a kid, when a girl would ask me to dance. Though I was the only wallflower in that particular corner, I still had to confirm that they meant me.

"You can't wait here any longer without getting a ticket!" The officer shouted. This time he was close enough that saying it at a normal volume would have sufficed; but, if there was one thing I knew, this was the most action some airport officers would see. So, they liked to punch it up a little. I don't know that I blame them. When I worked security at Salt Lake International, before the TSA took over, I had seen my share of odd escalations. The national guard had been always at the ready, armed with M4s behind every security checkpoint.

I resigned myself to the fact that I was going to have to circle the airport. I raised my hands in a surrendering gesture and turned to close the trunk. That was when a small man wearing very tattered clothes covered in dust approached. His wild beard was speckled with things I was hoping was dirt.

"Jared?" he asked.

"Dave?"

He offered a tired nod. Limping in his fabric shoes, he reached the vehicle. He clutched a black trash bag with some duct tape on it, and a very interesting curry smell was emanating from him. Dave stood at about five-foot-ten with brown hair. He had a slender frame and wore an unkept beard.

It reminded me of the scene from the movie *Tommy Boy* when Tommy Callahan, played by Chris Farley, extracted a black trash bag wrapped in duct tape from the baggage claim as his "luggage" after flying home from college.

The officer took a step closer to me. It was closer than I was comfortable with; I am pretty sure he ate pastrami for lunch.

"Are you sure that is your passenger?" The officer asked. He pointed, rudely, at the dusty man by my car.

"Yes," I said. It was a lie.

In reality, I had doubts about the person that was climbing into my vehicle. At that point I had settled on dealing with a stranger rather than the airport officer. I walked around to the driver's side and got in. I let out a deep sigh as I buckled up. Now the question on my mind was, what is this persons story?

"Dave," I opened, "how are you doing today?"

"I've been better," he said.

He coughed a bit and cleared his throat. I wondered if it was allergies or a cold. He was not at his best. This was before the era of COVID-19, so a cough didn't mean much.

"I hear you," I said. "It looks like we are headed up to Heber; is that right?"

"That is correct." He stifled a yawn.

It was always nice to do a ride further from the airport than downtown Salt Lake. Heber was by far one of the best fares I could have wished for. A ride of this type would typically yield five or six quick trips in Park City, where drivers were paid better, before I headed back into Salt Lake. On this occasion I would return to the airport just two rides later.

"Very good," I said.

With that, I eagerly escaped the hovering of the airport police officer. I glanced in the mirror, and I couldn't help but think that I was probably driving a homeless person to Heber. The curry smell was much stronger than I had anticipated.

"Just getting home or just visiting," I asked.

There was a long pause at the question. It was actually my standard question when picking someone up from the airport, but in this case, I think he was trying to size up if I was being a smartass.

He sagged into a deep sigh. "Just getting home."

"Welcome back," I said. "If you didn't know, there is a cold front coming in right behind this storm. You're probably going to see snow in Heber."

People always appreciated a good weather update, especially if they were just arriving in town. It was all part of my mathematical formula to maximize profit and reviews. Dress nice + drive nice + nice conversation + nice advice = higher percentage of five-star reviews and a decent tip. It wasn't a guarantee by any means: people in general are odd, and can be unpredictable.

"Ah, I didn't know that. Thank you for the tip," said Dave.

I nodded my head and continued to drive. With Heber about forty minutes ahead of us, I knew there would be time to chat some more. I wanted to be sure that I was courteous, but at the same time, I really wanted to know his story. What was in the trash bag, and why he was dressed so poorly. For a moment, I imagined the possibility that Dave was in fact a serial killer and we were now headed to the notorious second location.

"This is a good song," he said. It was Depeche Mode's "Enjoy the Silence." The comment interrupted my spiraling imagination, which was a healthy change. As a writer my imagination sometimes runs dark and vivid.

"Funny story, this was my favorite song growing up," I said. I had owned the song on tape recording from the radio, the music video on VHS, the single cassette, the album on cassette, the CD, and finally the digital file. To be candid, just listing that makes me feel as old as it sounds. Sheesh.

"Really?" His curiosity was refreshing. Most people don't ask.

"Yeah, I used to stay up on Saturday nights and watch music videos, because we didn't have cable to watch MTV. I always watched for this music video."

The thing I didn't say was that growing up in a house with six other siblings and only two TV's, there was typically a high demand for the color picture box, and there were three times I would fight to the death for. First was the Saturday night music video time (which I would eventually switch to MTV's 120 Minutes when cable was introduced to my family). Second was the coveted Saturday morning cartoons (I needed my He-Man, Inspector Gadget, and Thundercat's fix). Third, was weekday morning cartoons (G.I. Joe and Transformers). Duke, Snake-eyes, and Optimus Prime got me through my elementary school days. Fourth, my afternoon shows (A-Team and Air Wolf).

Oh, and anytime Top Gun was on.

I might have dominated the TV a little bit. In all fairness, I was the second oldest.

"I really like that video too, with the king walking over the hills with the lawn chair." Dave leaned forward with real interest. His knowledge on the topic was surprising. Ironically, his memory of the music video lines up with my kids, who are very, very tired of me mentioning that I stayed up to watch it when I was a kid.

"That's the one," I said, with probably a little too much excitement. I could sometimes connect with people, but a connection through this song was something special. Just thinking about the song actually brings back memories of hanging out with my good friend Roger Whiting and listening to similar bands like Erasure while playing video games.

I will keep from spiraling into another montage of my childhood. I just want to mention that Hero's Quest II and Prince of Persia would have played a big role in that dive.

"Hey man, can you do me a favor?" Dave asked. This was a common question I heard as a driver, and 99% of the time it was harmless.

"Sure," I said.

"Tell me, what did the cop say to you when I was getting in," he asked.

A little sigh of relief passed through me. His request was fair, and I could relate to his curiosity. "He was asking me if you were really my passenger."

"I guess I do look kind of rough, but still, kind of a jerk to ask."

"Yeah," I said. Not a full lie, but a partial one. Airport cops tended to be aggressive towards the rideshare community in particular. They liked threatening to issue tickets—sometimes as much as six thousand dollars—or to impound a vehicle, or to report us to our rideshare companies. Typically it was for things like parking too close to a crosswalk or waiting a minute too long for someone at the pickup zone.

One time, an officer told me that I had passed through the pickup zone too many times in too short of a span of time. For the record, I had been there four times, and it was in close sequence. But each visit was for a different passenger.

Not every airport officer was like that. Enough of them were, though, for the reputation to stick.

So, I didn't have tons of love for the airport cops. I would like to think that the officer was asking about my passenger for my safety and security.

"Did you have any doubts about picking me up?" Dave asked.

The blunt question caught me off guard, but I decided to go with the truth. "I have picked up all sorts from all over,; but to be honest, I wondered for a moment."

A nod and a chuckle from the back seat eased some of my tension. After all, he had just called the officer a jerk for thinking the same thing.

"Thank you for being honest," said Dave. "I'm actually getting back into town from doing service in Tibet."

I wanted to ask the tacky question of if he had seen "Seven Years in Tibet" with Brad Pitt, but I resisted. Instead, I opted for a different tacky question that he probably heard dozens of times. "Wow, that sounds amazing. How long were you there for?"

Really, my mind was flooded with dozens of other questions I wanted to ask, like, why?: Why? How? What happened?

"I was there for a year, but that is not entirely why I look like this," said Dave.

I didn't think that everyone came back from Tibet looking like Dave. I had just assumed he lived off service, generosity, or was on a spiritual quest or something.

"Oh?" This was the best that I could respond with. His answers stacked questions like a librarian's book recommendation list.

"On my way back from Tibet, I was unofficially detained in a different country that I won't mention. I was there for a few weeks. Then they conveniently 'misplaced' my luggage, but not this bag of what I suspect is clothes."

His answer didn't fully satisfy my curiosity, but I didn't think it wise to press him on it. Also, I mean, what the freak, who misplaces luggage with a trash bag?

"Holy crap! Are you okay?" I once again resisted asking another tacky question, like, have you ever seen "The Terminal" with Tom Hanks.

"Physically, I think so…"

Instantly I thought of the first Iron Man movie and decided try for subtle humor. "Do you need anything? A bottle of water? A hamburger?"

Immediately after, I wondered if he had even seen Iron Man. At least it came off as friendly.

"Thanks for offering, I will be. I'm good, just want to get home and into my own bed," he said.

"I can imagine," I agreed. In reality, the closest I could come to relating was a week of Boy Scouts camping at camp Geronimo in Arizona. I had been overjoyed to return home and pass out on my own, soft, familiar bed—and that had only been a single week.

"I just got that, by the way, that was funny. Because Tony Stark asked for a hamburger when he got back from captivity," said Dave.

I grinned. So far the things I knew about this guy were: he did service in countries like Tibet, had great taste in music, had seen Iron Man, he was detained in an unlisted country, was given a trash bag for luggage, and his ratty clothes were not by choice.

"You got me," I said.

Dave had liked my music, gotten my humor, and was open to having great conversation. This was a guy, I thought, with great groundwork for a friendship. Then again, there were so many more variables that could still mean he was a serial killer, or a government spy, or a hitman, or okay so my imagination was spiraling again.

"Do you have a family?" he asked.

This was an odd shift from where the conversation was. Most likely he didn't want to talk more about his traumatic experience—or he was he trying to decide if people would notice if I went missing. (Probably not. But, you know, spiraling imagination.)

"Yes. Five kids, and an amazing wife." I knew this answer would get his attention. It garnered responses from everyone. My favorite response was from Tera Strong at the Salt Lake FanX convention, when in the voice of "Teen Titans" character Raven she said, "Five kids, somebody is crazy!" It was awesome.

"Five! Five kids?!"

His response made me think of Jeremy Piven's character Paul in the movie, "Grosse Pointe Blank," when he asked John Cusack's character, "Ten years?"

"Yup," I answered proudly. At the same time I realized that I watch way too many movies, and TV shows, and web series, and okay all things media.

"No wonder you drive for rideshare," said Dave.

Normally, this is where I would talk about my son being on the transplant list. Not for pity, but because most people could relate to the stress of hospital bills and struggling family members. Dave had just spent weeks detained in a foreign airport. I decided on a different tack. "Three of them are teenagers," I said. "It makes things interesting."

"Wow."

I liked when someone would ask about my kids, because it made asking about their personal life fair game. "Do you have any kids?"

"No, but it wasn't from a lack of effort. Things just didn't work out."

"Sorry to hear that." I had known other people in situations like this, and I have never figured out the best response to a situation like this. It always leaves me grateful for my kids, teenagers and heart transplants and all.

It makes me feel lucky.

"Thanks," said Dave. "I think that is why I do a lot of service around the world. It gets my mind off of everyday stuff we take for granted and gives me a way to make the world a better place."

He kind of trailed off at the end, and for a good amount of time he just stared out the window thoughtfully. I wondered if that would end the conversation for the rest of the drive. That is, until the radio switched to Jack Johnson's "Better Together."

"You know how Jack Johnson seems like a cool guy in his videos and things?" Dave asked.

"Yeah?" Another shift in conversation. It seemed pretty random, but I suspect that he also felt as though the silence was awkward.

"As it turns out, he is even nicer in person," said Dave.

"That is cool." It was always really neat to meet a celebrity or to hear about one that is down to Earth and appreciates things. Having been a special guest at FanX, I had the opportunity to meet many famous people in person. The vast majority were amazing and personable. Henry Winkler actually gave everyone a hug that came to get his autograph. It was priceless to see my mother hug the Fonzie from "Happy Days." Once again, that was pre-Covid.

Tragically enough, some people are not very nice; but we won't mention those experiences here.

"Trust me, I have met my share of famous, over-the-top ungrateful personalities, but Jack stands out to me. He is someone that seems well-rounded. Did you know he was a professional surfer for a min?"

"I didn't." This was really a fun fact that I had no idea about. It was right up there with hearing Katee Sackhoff tell me about her mother being a teacher and her father being a construction worker.

"Yeah, an accident took that away. Still such a nice guy."

"For sure," I said.

Ironically, like Jack Johnson, Katee had been pursuing a career as a swimmer until she suffered an injury.

"Anyways, on this next turn there will be a gate with a guard. I will talk with the guard," said Dave. He leaned forward and sort of pointed a direction. This was very common behavior from passengers, even when the map was showing the same thing.

"Sounds good," I said.

Gated communities weren't new, but the majority of the time there was a guard shack and no actual guard. This guard post was massive. And it was manned by not one person, but two.

"Can I help you?" The guard asked. He reached back and rested his hand on an item attached to his belt. I could see that it wasn't a gun but didn't want to find out if it was a taser or pepper spray. These guys were serious about their jobs.

"Hey Frank," Dave waved from the back seat. He rolled the window behind me down a little.

"Dave?"

"The one and only."

"Code?"

"Never rains in July."

A code like that seemed absurd to me. I mean, the guard recognized him. I couldn't help but wonder if that was one of those codes that, now that I had heard it, I wouldn't be able to leave this place ever again. (It was not.) Then it dawned on me: what if the code was to let the guards know if he was being taken to his house against his will.

"It is good to see you, sir." The guard relaxed his stance. "The prep team should be finished for your arrival."

The moment I heard prep team, I thought of it as a military term. Maybe this guy was a spy or something. I figured it was best not to ask.

"Perfect. Thank you," said Dave.

The guard gate slid open and allowed us to drive forward. It didn't take long before I was surrounded by what, in my mind, I would estimate as multi-million-dollar homes. I noticed that at the front driveway of each house was a massive stone or sign that named the property. Things like Dragon's Den, Mercedes Bend, Asgard, etc.

"These houses are impressive," I said. I was gawking at that point, as we were driving only twenty miles per hour. I imagined a prep team for a house like this wasn't just a maid service.

"I am fortunate: there are a lot of good people here when they are here," Dave said. There was a little bit of a sad tone in his voice.

"How often are they here?" Instantly, I thought, I could watch these houses for them while they are gone. My guess is they already have people that do that.

"Oh, it depends on the various families. How large the family is, how much they want to impress their friends, what kind of drama is going on. Regardless, not much," he said.

"That is too bad. If I lived here, I don't know how often I would leave."

"If you lived here, you would have the resources to go to all the most beautiful places on Earth. I suspect you would travel."

"You're right, I probably would."

"Oh, on this next turn you are going to reach another gate."

I thought he was joking. Until I reached the gate. This time there was no guard. I pulled up to a panel that had a keypad and what looked like a fingerprint scanner. After a moment, the gate opened. The app guided me to the first house. My guess was that this one was worth a lot more than the other houses. It reminded me of a place where I think Tony Stark would live.

"Where would you like for me to drop you off?"

I had to ask because it looked like there were several spots that would make sense. Though I figured the five-car garage on the left was not going to be one of them.

"Right here is good."

"Thank you so much for choosing rideshare." This was my standard exit saying. It was also sort of a plea to rate me as a driver. I offered my best, 'please help me feed my five kids' look.

"Thank you, it was most welcome after my last three weeks." I could tell he really meant the statement. He paused for a moment almost like he wanted to say something else.

"I hope you get some good rest," I offered. This was a genuine wish for Dave.

"You know what, hold on a second," he said.

He exited the vehicle and walked into the house. After a few minutes, he came back to the vehicle. With a big grin on his face, he extended his hand with a business-size envelope. I rolled down the window, and he offered it to me.

"Good luck with the teenagers. You're a good person," he said.

"Oh, my gosh. Thank you so much!" I said, gawking at the envelope. I thought for sure Dave was a hitman. The envelope was thick.

"Don't mention it," he said. Dave walked back to his house, and I drove away. Even without Dave in the vehicle, the strong smell of curry remained. I took my time admiring the houses some more on my way out. I, of course, was freaking out a little that I had an envelope of money sitting on the passenger seat. I normally slid cash tips into my suit coat pocket. I stopped for a second to look through the envelope. It was fifty dollars in one-dollar bills.

I changed my mind again; Dave wasn't a hitman; he was for sure just a super nice guy.

As I approached the entrance with the guards, one of the guards prompted me to stop. This was a first for me as well. On the way out of such places I had never been stopped before.

"Hey, what is your name?" the guard asked me. I was speechless for a moment at the unusual question.

"Jared." I hesitated. I mean, was this where they decided to 'take care' of me? Had Dave call the security checkpoint and changed his mind on the envelope of money?

"It looks like it took you a while to get from Dave's place to here. What were you doing?"

"I was just driving carefully," I said. A somewhat truth: driving slowly is driving safe, after all. I wondered how they handled pizza delivery people, or delivery people in general. Maybe they wanted to make sure I wasn't plotting to break into someone's house. After all, this was legit security for a wealthy community.

"Uh-huh, well, drive safe out there," said the guard. I could hear his skepticism.

"Yes sir."

He signaled for the gate to open. I had just passed through the gate when I got a prompt for another ride request, as I had hoped. I watched in my mirror to see what the guards were doing as I pulled away. Sure, enough, they were watching me intently.

I had to give them props for the attention to detail. Another one of my side gigs was working as security for Real Salt Lake, where I had been given credit for being a top security screener and for my attention to detail.

I couldn't shake how wild the ride was, from thinking I had picked up a homeless person, to dropping off a billionaire. Not to mention having had the chance to enter a gated community within a gated community.

Bunnies Vs. Unicorns

Rideshare had promoted Halloween as one of the most successful nights of the year to drive. As it turned out, I, apparently like all the other Rideshare drivers in Salt Lake City, planned to work it. With my financial situation the way it was, I needed to take advantage of every good driving opportunity. I was really bummed to be out driving for Halloween, as this was the first year since my children were old enough to trick or treat that I wasn't out with them.

I had a strategy. I was going to stick near the Avenues and the University of Utah as much as possible. It was my theory that there would be a lot of party hopping by college students; and for the most part, I was right. Lots of extra rides meant hitting the bonus and a better chance for tips. Late night and early morning passengers liked to express more gratitude, and not just because of inebriants—though that was, sometimes, a factor.

Earlier in the day, I had taken several college students to parties on and off the University of Utah campus. Even those headed to their first party seemed to already have had a few drinks to get things started. There were a couple that were already completely smashed.

Right in the middle of the driving night, I was summoned to a house down a very narrow street. Cars lined both sides of the road. It was difficult for cars to squeeze past each other down the center. For sanity's sake, the street would have been better as a one-way.

I don't say this lightly. I lived in upstate New York for two years, where one-way streets are common. They're nonsensical. I don't like them. But if a street is going to be narrow, one-way is sometimes better.

For anyone who hasn't driven near the University of Utah, I highly recommend Google Mapping it to see some of the comical street sizes. Then imagine cars parked on both sides of the street and vehicles trying to pass each other in opposite directions. I worried about hitting someone's mirror. Or a pedestrian walking into the road between two vehicles without looking.

As I approached the pickup point, I noticed six police cars with the lights on and several officers working on breaking up what looked like a massive party. There was a crowd of people standing on lawns and walking towards the street, probably looking for their rideshares.

I noticed a group of six college students wearing matching outfits, which barely qualified as a costume let alone classified it as clothes. Each wore a headband with bunny ears and had a little white cotton ball tail attached to the back of the very, very skimpy outfit. As they approached, I could tell that they were looking hard at the Journey for confirmation that this was the right vehicle. The leader of the group looked down at her phone and back at my vehicle a few times.

I shook my head at their costumes. The clothes left absolutely nothing to the imagination. Based on the way they carried themselves—bubbly attitudes, enthusiasm dialed to eleven—and their athletic physiques, I suspected they were either cheerleaders or on a dance team. It was a snap judgement; they aligned closely with film depictions of college girls in similar getups.

The girls were giggly, and eager to reach the car. Normally, I would get out to open the doors for them, but there was no place to park. I rolled down the window. The leader, six-foot-two and blonde, leaned into the passenger window. This was even *more* revealing; she did not seem to care. I was not impressed by her lackadaisical attitude.

She held out her phone so I could see the screen. "Jared?" she asked, bright enough to be off-putting.

"Yes. Steph, right?" I answered.

"That's me!" She smiled widely. At that moment one of the parked cars pulled into the crowded traffic, which opened a place to put the Journey.

"I'm going to pull forward up here," I told her.

"Sounds good!"

With careful, surgical accuracy, I pulled into the open spot. Then I jumped out to help the six scanty women into the car. To access the back row of seats, I slid the middle seat forward like a drawer. Impressed Oh!'s of appreciation sounded from the group. Two of the women clapped like I'd performed a magic trick. All of them smelled like alcohol.

They cheered again once they were loaded in and ready to go, and I closed the door. Other drivers trying to squeeze their cars through the narrow road were rapidly losing their patience. I needed to be quick about getting out.

"Okay," I said, buckling my seatbelt, "it looks like we aren't far from your destination."

"Sounds right," Steph said. Voices raised at the other five girls chatted and giggled at volume. I felt like I needed subtitles to follow the overlapping conversations. Sort of like, I thought, watching anime at home.

"Oh! You're adorable," said Steph. "Can I get a picture with you?"

I was in my suit and the fedora. It was a request I got often. So many people had worn my hat for a quick picture that I sometimes wondered if the hat should have its own Instagram.

"Sure," I said. Traffic wasn't really moving anyways, crowded as the street was. She held up her phone and leaned towards the middle console of the Journey. Her fingers folded into a peace sign.

"Girls, picture!" she said. Then she fired off several quick snaps on her phone.

I focused on escaping the street. It was a relief to make it to the main road. Away from the dangerous combination of tight traffic and milling pedestrians—*drunk* milling pedestrians—I had enough bandwidth to pay more attention to my passengers. All things considered, it wasn't a conversation I had expected.

"You're totes wrong," a girl was saying. "The series doesn't need those movies."

"I'm with you," said another. "The series it whack until you get to the middle of the set."

"Well *I* think you're all cray-cray," said Steph. "The franchise needs the first three; it makes it a fuller story."

"I don't care for any but the most recent ones, to be honest," said one of the girls in the very back.

This drew the ire of her friends. "Now *that* is cray," a couple declared.

"Wait! I know how to settle this. Once and for all," announced Steph.

The vehicle quieted. The five other girls focused on Stephanie. I admit that I was also curious: to understand what exactly they were arguing over, and how she planned to resolve it.

"Our driver Jared has a Salt Lake FanX special guest pass hanging from his rearview mirror," Steph told them. "He has the answer."

I floundered. I'm always willing to converse with rideshare passengers, but I was unprepared to be dragged into this one. I still wasn't sure what they were talking about. I didn't see how the guest pass could be related.

It did make me laugh, a little, thinking that my conference contact Blake Casselman might sometimes be in the same boat. Also, at the girls' confidence in me knowing the answer. FanX represented a billion different fandoms, spanning anime to video games to movies to comics to beyond. My side of it was mostly writing and video games. I worried that their interest was in something like anime, which I knew little about.

Well. Unless it was Tri-gun, or anything from Miyazaki. Fun fact: the first real anime I ever watched was "Nausicaa of the Valley of the Wind."

"Yeah," chimed several of the girls. "Let's see what Jared has to say."

It was flattering that they wanted to know. I still didn't know what they were arguing over. And the group was already divided; there was no way to avoid the argument unscathed.

"So," said Steph. "Tell us honestly. What do you think of Star Wars episodes one, two, and three? And are they necessary to the franchise."

It caught me off guard. More than I was before, at least. Star Wars. Not an anime. Not something young and hip and cool; not something cutesy and fun. Star Wars. *Old* Star Wars.

I was abruptly grateful that they wanted an opinion, too, rather than a definitive answer on something in-verse. Unlike today, I did not have Star Wars diehard Bryan Young on speed dial.

As a child who'd watched "Return of the Jedi" in the theater, who'd stood in lines for the subsequent Star Wars movies as they were released: I had this.

"The first three episodes get a bad rap," I said. "They complete the series. I stood in line for hours for Episode One. You had to, to get a good seat; assigned seating wasn't a thing yet. Watching them in the machete order might improve your opinion, though, because the storytelling aligns better with audience expectations."

Well. I'd dated myself by talking about movies pre-assigned-seating. It identified me as either the older, outdated clone trooper generation, or equally older but much more likeable Wise Jedi. But it wasn't like I could go into it in depth: I was driving. Good drivers watch the road.

"Yeah, but that excludes Episode One," said Steph. "Episode One is the superglue that brings everything together."

I was delighted by her instant engagement and her passion for the subject. Also, I was floored. She knew exactly what the machete order was. She had *opinions*. She had not seemed to me, on first impression, to be the sort of person with strong opinions about the machete order of Star Wars.

In retrospect, I wish I'd asked more about her stance. I want to know why she thought Episode One was superglue.

"Episode One is optional in the machete order," I agreed, "but I recommend keeping it in."

(Ironically: I've had this conversation many times—at events, at work, at parties—but never at Salt Lake FanX. Who'd figure.)

The girls sat in silence more a moment, thinking it over. I suspected they'd heard this before; I wasn't adding anything new to a well-hashed discussion. Then a girl in the very back said, "But Jar Jar. And pod racing."

"Yup. Both played vital roles in the movies. After all, it was Jar Jar who voted Palpatine into power. And the pod racing was to introduce the idea of the force enhancing inborn skill," I said. "Plus there's that rumor that Lucas had more in store for Jar Jar, like being a Sith."

I was parroting speculation and conjecture. I should have been more curious; I regret that I didn't pursue this line of analysis, either. Why Jar Jar specifically? Why pod racing? But in that moment, I was thinking of other problems with the movie that—I believed—were worse. Jar Jar and pod racing were fruit that hung too low for debate.

"Blasphemy," a voice from the back said.

"I really think they wasted an amazing opportunity by killing off Darth Maul in Episode One," Steph said. This was an opinion that I was totally behind, and I nodded in agreement. To this day, I feel that Lucas's creating of Darth Maul was one the greatest gifts to the Star Wars universe, but at the same time is his most underdeveloped character.

"Uh, correction, Darth Maul is alive and well in Rebels and Solo," another girl chimed in.

"I think saying alive and well is stretching it a little bit,; he is only half the man he once was," a different girl argued.

"You mean half the Dathomiri, he once was," a girl in the back said. The other girls broke out in wild laughter.

It was in this moment that the surrealism hit. I was driving a vehicle of "sexy college bunnies," collected from a Halloween party shut down by the police, to *another* late-night party near campus—while they debated one of the iconic cores of sci-fi geekdom. *In detail.* The fact that one of them casually name-dropped Darth Maul's race was pretty hard core. Most Star Wars fans couldn't tell you something like that. I've been an avid fan of Star Wars since the theater release, and I couldn't tell you something like that, either.

My first opinion of the women hadn't been great. And it was completely wrong.

"You know what I mean; they should have used Maul in more of the series, don't you think?" Steph asked.

"I completely agree. Not just from a Sith interaction, but Ray Park is phenomenal and would have contributed a lot more to the movie. Maybe he will in the sequel to Solo," I said. I realized that I was possibly out of my depth a little, but I was pleased to have dropped Ray Park's name. Had to recover my street cred as a geek, you know?

"Maybe, but to be honest since we know that Obi-Wan kills him on Tatooine," a girl began. Which made me want to bring in his role in Solo, fan speculation on the sequel, and Maul's role in Rebels. And then the phone chimed from the Journey's dashboard.

"It looks like we have arrived at your destination," I announced.

"Aw, the conversation was just getting good," Steph said. For me, the conversation had been great from the beginning.

"Well, if you come out to FanX, we can continue the conversation," I said.

"Actually, I was thinking we could just keep going. Could you drive us around the block?" Steph asked. "If that's okay with everyone?"

"Yeah! Let's keep talking," the other women in the vehicle chimed in.

"Sure," I said. This group of women had managed to surprise me yet again.

"So, tell us, how did you end up being a special guest at FanX?" Steph asked.

"Yeah, wow, that is a great story," I said. "I was fortunate enough to have written about the 49ers and Utah Jazz in the past, and I had just published my second book *Changing Wax*. I got an opportunity to be on a panel with some of the most amazing people I know. It had Dan Wells, Larry Correa, Natalie Whipple, Dan Willis, and Johnny Worthen. It was about Bad Writing Advice," I said.

"Wait, so you're an author?" someone in the back asked.

"Yeah, I have a couple of books and some short stories published," I answered.

"Which book of yours would you recommend?"

"I would recommend *Changing Wax*. . It is a fantasy comedy like Terry Pratchett and Douglas Adams," I said.

"Oh my gosh! I love the *Discworld* and *Hitchhikers Guide to the Universe*! I have to get this book right now!" Steph said.

"So do I!" a couple more of them said.

"Which Pratchett book is your favorite?" Steph asked.

"That is a hard thing to answer, but I have to go with Jingo," I said.

"The Commander Vimes series is brilliant," she said.

"I love Mort!" The passenger in the far back added.

"Come on, hands down the Moist von Lipwig is the best," another of the passengers said.

"I love them all, but always look forward to Lord Vetinari," another said.

"Do you read any Neil Gaiman?" Steph asked.

I felt a tad ashamed. I'd had Neil on my list forever, but had never actually read any of his books. Actually, more recently, Charlie N. Holmberg's books had been occupying my reading list. I had just finished her *Paper Magician* series. Which, fun fact, was optioned once to Disney for a movie.

"No, I need to. I've been going through a really odd selection of books, from Tom Clancy to Clive Cussler, to Terry Pratchett and Charlie N. Holmberg," I said.

"Right?!" Then I asked, "I am curious: what is everyone majoring in?"

They went on to list that couple of them were in Engineering, a couple in Legal areas, and the rest happened to be in similar programs around Psychology.

So, it was hitting me hard at this point: this group of passengers are into reading, are true Star Wars fans, are students at the University of Utah, and dress like sexy bunnies. I was feeling both excited about the group that had destroyed my assumptions, and I was feeling ashamed that I had prebuilt an assumption like that in the first place.

We had arrived, again, at their destination.

"I totally want to keep chatting, but we have friends waiting on us inside," Steph said.

"Just remember, if you want to keep chatting, stop by FanX. This is the same suit I will be wearing," I said.

"I don't suppose you want to come inside and hang out for a little bit?" Steph asked.

"Oh, that would be so cool!" a passenger agreed.

"Yeah, come in," another said.

"I wish I could. I need to keep driving for the night; gotta pay the bills and keep the family fed," I said.

"I totally respect that," Steph said.

I got out and helped them exit the vehicle. A group of people came out of the house to greet them. I overheard one of the bunny girls announce to the reception party: "We had the best driver I have ever met!"

As I climbed back into the Journey, Steph offered a big wave and shouted, "May the force be with you!"

"May the force be with you!" I replied back.

I have hoped to see them again, but to this date, I have not run into them again.

Of all the many passengers I have had, I have only had a couple of Star Wars conversations. That one was one of my all-time favorites. The lesson to take away from this ride: don't assume anything from age, gender, or dress; and obviously, the first three episodes were important. Also, the ride made me appreciate the amazing people behind FanX.

It was thanks to my involvement in the conference as a special guest that I got involved in the Star Wars debate at all.

Driving at Sundance

I picked up a cute middle-aged couple,
From the crowded Kimble Junction shuffle.
I was greeted by one offering boisterous laughter,
And the other clearly thinking that I was riffraff.

As we headed for the Sundance packed park city,
The conversation in the backseat developed into something less
    than pretty.
The first said "Listen I thought her performance was absolutely
    brilliant."
The second replied "Well I can tell you my patience is not that
    resilient."

"What did you think of the supporting actor's performance?"
"I would say their style is all conformance."
"Surely there is something about that movie we can agree on."
"Yes, I am positive that we would both say it was way too long."

As we arrived at circle of the lodge hotel,
I acted as if standing on eggshell.
"Thanks for getting us here safe and sound."
"I would say your driving was good enough that I hope to see you
    around."

I watched the couple depart to into the large structure
and wondered if there was further lecture.
The next day I saw a review come across my phone,
it was by none other than the critic
Who wrote on the conformance overtone.

Oh, Drunk Dave

I once had a very drunk passenger named Dave,
who wondered which sports team was my fav.
The 49ers, I answered his slurred question,
"The 49ers, ha," he started the lecture session.

"They haven't been good since Jordan retired."
I offered a quizzical look to Dave clearly tired.
"Are you talking about the Bulls?" I promptly asked,
hoping the follow up would spark his memory of the past.

"No," he sputtered with a dramatic wave of the hand,
"You know it is people like you that brought Pablo to power" he
        attempted to expand.
"People are not what they seem" he said somewhat alertly,
"the government is everywhere, hidden in plain sight so covertly."

Finally, I reached Dave's drop off location after the lengthy
        education,
still trying to figure out his mental destination.
"I want to make sure this is where you wanted to be dropped off."
"Of course it is, do I look like an idiot" he said as he slid out of
        the car like a sloth

As I drove away, I got pinged to pick up the same drunk Dave,
I turned around and pulled up with a wave.
He climbed into the car with a deep sigh,
"The last driver I had dropped me off at the wrong house."
Painting me as a bad guy.

Just three houses down was the new drop off point,
I let him out and watched him to walk to the setpoint.

I wish Dave the best of luck on his future rides,
and to whoever provides.

Ode to Gina the Nurse

Near the end of a long Rideshare driving run,
Long after the sky turned dark after the fall of the sun.
I once picked up a woman whose name was Gina,
Who grew up in the distant country of Argentina.

Before I could offer a friendly greeting,
She started to talk with no breaks even for breathing.
Thank you so much for coming to get me,
I don't have a car because I live life carefree.

I always use Rideshare to get into work,
I prefer the people I deal with especially the clerk.
I opened my mouth to ask a follow up question,
But I was quickly shut when I realized she had not yet finished her
      talking session.

I nodded my head at her thoughts on how to save to world,
Which promptly changed to talking about video games that take
      place in the netherworld.
Impressed at her speaking speed and stamina,
As well as her in-depth knowledge on Canada.

As we approached the drop off destination,
She did not stop, slow, or offer hesitation.
Finally, she started to close down the conversation,
After telling me about all of her jobs since her high school
      graduation.

She exited the car with a quick goodbye,
And in my many rides I have not seen such a rare social butterfly.

Logistics

For me, logistics is just as fascinating a topic as any. It consists of things like the app, the map directions, the pickup spot, finding the best gas stations, and playing Tetris with luggage. The first time I turned on the app, I had little idea as to what would happen. I knew it would assign me a passenger, and then I would go pick them up, then drop them off. I didn't know that it wouldn't show me where I would be taking people until I arrived to pick up the passenger. I could be headed right down the street, or an hour away.

On my very first passenger pickup, I was not only super nervous, but when I arrived I immediately selected the button to call the passenger. Later I found that it is best to wait to call them until you have been there for the wait period. This is because they are notified when you arrive, and if you call them right away, people get annoyed. Thankfully my first passenger, Jimmy, was super cool. All we did was talk about the Marvel Universe the entire time.

Imagine how amazing it is to get paid for a five-minute ride you are giving someone when the conversation goes like this:

Jimmy: "Dude, do you like the Marvel Universe?"

Me: "Woah, I love the Marvel Universe."

Jimmy: "Sweet! Oh man, I totally hope there is an X-Man crossover like the comic books."

Me: "Dude, totally! I just hope they have Gambit in there."

Jimmy: "Gambit is the man! That would be totally killer!"

Ok, so the conversation was a lot less Bill and Ted than that, but you get the point. Depending on the drop off point, most conversations are either speed dating, a marathon (pace yourself), or Simon Says. The last one is a ride where there is no conversation, they just issue orders.

Most of the time the app would show me the best route to my passenger. Occasionally something was off. For instance, the passenger would manage to input the pickup at their home address, when actually they were at a restaurant. Other times, the passenger lived in an area with little to no good cell coverage, which resulted in the app getting close, but not to the right place. That was often true of large apartment complexes. Sometimes passengers would send the rideshare to pick up a friend, which has its own complications.

Of course, it was always fun when I picked someone up who demanded that I take a different route than the directions on the app. More often than not, the app would have good reason to divert us from a common freeway or road; but when a passenger demands it, I do what they request. Often the passenger end up paying me more.

During one such instance, I picked up a family from the airport and was driving them to West Jordan. It should have been a straight shot with no reason to divert out of our way to the main freeway. The passenger was as confused as I was, and they let me know they wanted to go the shortest route possible. As it turns out there was a massive accident and a tanker full of fuel was blocking all of the lanes and on fire. We ended up spending an additional 45 minutes waiting in traffic. The passenger apologized to me several times.

One point of annoyance is that parents will sometimes order rideshares for their underaged children. It is against policy for drivers to give rides to unaccompanied minors. I feel bad for the kids that I turned down because they were obviously underage; I have to remind myself that it is their parent that was unable to make better arrangements. I wouldn't feel too bad though, as most of the kids I turned rides down to were in very, very wealthy neighborhoods.

At the same time, there is a policy that we are not to ask people what their age is. This puts drivers in very questionable situations, where a high school student might be 18 and use the service unaccompanied. Also, some people in their twenties look like they could be in their teens. It is at the discretion of the driver to carry out the policy.

The most interesting rides were always picking someone up from a concert, sporting event, or other some such. One time I picked up a couple from a wedding party. I confirmed the name Erin and the destination: their home in Sandy. As we started driving away, I was flagged down by another of the wedding guests. I figured that my passenger had forgotten something. As it turns out, there was another person named Erin who had also called for a ride. The other person also lived in Sandy. They only reason they knew is because they had paid attention to the type of vehicle that was coming for them. The two women knew each other and exchanged a pretty good laugh over it.

There was another time I was picking up a large group up from Pierpont Avenue. Clubs, bars, and restaurants are the bulk of the businesses in the immediate area. The narrow two-lane street was packed that night. The police were camped at the exit of the parking garage administering breathalyzer tests to everyone driving out of there. Utah has the lowest legal blood alcohol threshold in the country. As I reached the middle of the street, I saw no less than a dozen rideshare drivers searching for passengers like I was.

A person knocked on my window and asked if I was looking for Todd. I told them that I was, and his group poured into the vehicle. The drive was fairly short, but due to demand the payout for me was very high. As I reached the destination, Todd asked me to drive over an extra block and make a turn. This was a little unusual, but not the first time the app had the destination off. I dropped the group off, then I got a call from the rideshare customer support. They wanted to verify the ride I just finished, and let me know they thought the passenger was a group that had hijacked someone else's ride.

Of all the rides I gave, the wedding mix-up and the Pierpont ride were the only two where I got the passengers wrong. I had a near miss at a bar on 1st South in Salt Lake, where two guys were helping a very drunk guy to the vehicle. They almost had him inside when my real passenger showed up.

When driving an XL-size vehicle, getting the passenger correct is oftentimes the least of your concerns. I can't tell you how many times passengers would order a ride for six people with luggage for six people on top of that. This is a quick conversation from one of my favorite attempts to fit six people and all of their bags:

It was a rented house in Park City. Their mountain of luggage waited outside with them. Some of the group looked like they'd managed to sneak in one last run on the slopes. All of them were young: no older than 23, tops. I got out to greet them. The name on the request was Frank.

Me: "Hello! I am looking for Frank?"

Frank: "That's me."

Me, as I opened the trunk of the Dodge Journey: "Awesome. It looks like we are headed to the airport, right?"

Frank: "Yup."

One of the others: "Um, Frank, is everything going to fit?"

Frank: "Jared, the app said the vehicle has room for six."

Me: "It does."

Frank: "What about our luggage?"

Me: "Great question. None of our vehicles have room for six people *and* six people's luggage, especially if there are snowboards involved."

One of the others: "What are we going to do, Frank, I can't miss my flight."

Frank: "Yes, I am aware. We're all on the same flight."

Me: "What I would recommend is that I take all of your luggage and who whoever can fit, and head to the airport. You can call a regular rideshare for the whoever's left."

Frank: "Ugh, this doesn't make any sense, how did we all get up here with our stuff?"

One of the others: "We all arrived at different times."

Frank: "Fine, lets load up the luggage, and see who we can fit."

One of the others: "Who is paying for the other ride?"

All of the others: "Not me!"

Frank: "You're kidding, right? You are all headed to Europe next week."

One of the others: "True, but I am trying to spend money on my credit cards to show that I am being responsible."

Frank: "FINE! I will pay for it. Geez."

I got the luggage loaded up pretty quick with room for two people to ride.

Frank: "Your ride will be here in five minutes."

Frank climbed into the passenger seat, and another person got in.

One of the others: "Wait, did you do a regular ride?"

Frank: "Yes."

One of the others: "Can you upgrade it to an XL, I mean there are four of us that have to ride all together."

Frank: "…"

Frank closed the door. "Okay, Jared, let's go."

On one occasion, I managed to fit five people (three kids and two adults) and all of their luggage for their ski trip destination of Park City from the airport. It was very tricky and uncomfortable for the adults, but we got it done.

There were several instances where the passengers called for a second vehicle when they saw mine. Funny enough, most of the time I simply transported all of the luggage to the destination while all of the passengers went in the other vehicle.

On the flip side, I did have one person call for an XL because they had just purchased a 55" TV. They were confident that it wouldn't fit in a regular rideshare. Once we got the TV in, I had to figure out how to fit the passenger's bike in as well. The looks we were getting from people, were priceless. That was the most interesting ride I gave from a Best Buy.

The heaviest suitcases I ever loaded into the Journey were for an amazing couple from India. They visit home just once every few years due to cost and distance. So, they had their suitcases jam packed with gifts for family members and friends. The suitcases each weighed exactly 100lbs. That was the maximum weight permitted for checked bags on the aircraft, and each bag came with a hefty $200 fee as well (from the airline, not me). Interesting fact: the flight time to India from Salt Lake is 33–37 hours, with a preferred route is through Europe. Similar to Tom Hanks' movie, "The Terminal," at any layover they have on the way to India, they are restricted to the airport terminal, and cannot venture out.

Huh. That is the second time I have referenced that movie in this book. I think I need to rewatch it.

It was during many of those drives that I learned more about Bollywood movies. I hadn't had any exposure to them prior, and found out that they are notorious for being lengthy epics, with lots of music. The average runtime for a Bollywood film is at over two hours.

I have helped load everything from lawn chairs, to skis, DJ equipment, a ladder, sports gear, computer equipment, and even things like cases of BDSM equipment. Fun fact: it turns out Salt Lake hosts an annual BDSM conference. I had the privilege of driving one of the keynote speakers, a psychologist specializing in Cognitive Psychology. That was a fascinating conversation; at the end of it, though, they requested that I not share the details.

It didn't take long before I developed a routine that helped ensure success. Pull up to the pickup point, and quickly evaluate: are there several people, do the people have luggage, bags, packages, groceries, or other items that they might need assistance with. If they have anything with them, I always jump out and promptly offer assistance.

Here are a couple of fun stories that highlight interesting logistical challenges.

The Fab Five

There was a call for an XL ride, only a few minutes away. The address took me to the storefront of a cute little sandwich shop. I pulled up to the curb, parked, and hit the button on the app to let my passengers know I was there. Then I waited for them to show.

Six people exited the shop. Five of them were very tall. The last one was even taller. All of them headed straight for my car.

Nervously, I exited the vehicle. There were enough people that we'd need the back row, which invariably meant showing off the sliding seat in the middle. If they got in. This was the first time I was truly concerned that the passengers might cancel due to the size of the vehicle. It could carry six (besides myself), but it was not built to carry people that tall.

"Bryan?" I asked the general group.

"Yup, that's us, bro," said one of them. Bryan, presumably.

A knot formed in my stomach. I opened the back door, deciding to get this over with like ripping off a band aid, and slid the seat forward to reveal the back row. Instead of the *Oohs* and *Ahhs* that I normally got, all I heard was loud laughter.

I wasn't surprised. I smiled and fake laughed along, pretending like I didn't know why they were laughing.

"Well, I picked up the rideshare, so I get shotgun," Bryan announced. "You'll have to stuff Dwayne in the back."

"You've got to be kidding me," said the exceptionally tall one. Evidently Dwayne. "Make Markus, Dave, or George."

I knew things were going to get interesting. Dwayne had to be in the range of seven-foot-something; the other four were all at least six-foot-five. Even with my mad Tetris skills, I couldn't imagine how they would fit.

At that moment, mind working over the puzzle, I noticed their shoes. All six pairs were expensive high top basketball shoes; only one pair was actually tied.

"Nah, man, the middle will have less room," said Markus.

"How so?" Dwayne asked. There was serious concern in his voice. I was trying hard to imagine the center folded up in the back. I worried that they would break or sprain something trying to make it work. I actually wondered what vehicle had brought them to the shop in the first place.

"You'll get the seat all to yourself, so you can turn sideways," Bryan said. They all looked at each other, thinking. When no one disputed his logic, Dwayne crawled into the back. He turned sideways as advertised to fit. His knees ended up next to his ears.

It reminded me of the classic Transformers cartoon, from the 1980's. A handful of the Decepticons folded into cassettes rather than vehicles, and were then carried around by Soundwave (who turned into, you guessed it, a boombox). Side note: Soundwave was my favorite Decepticon in the show.

The others climbed in and were just as crammed as you would imagine. We tried several variations of sliding seats backwards and forwards. We leaned seats back and angled people as best we could to get the doors shut.

I let out a huge sigh of relief the moment we got onto the road and headed to our destination. A moving can of sardines or clowns. I could tell that at least four of the five wore a very similar cologne, partly because there was very little air left in the vehicle. It was pretty cold outside, so no one was about to roll down a window.

"You are looking sharp my man," Bryan said.

"Thanks," I replied. This time I was wearing my dark navy-blue suit and red paisley tie. This was one of my favorite combinations, especially since in the middle of the red tie was a golden tie tack sent to me by the President of the United States for volunteer work.

"I gotta ask, who is your favorite basketball team in Utah?" Bryan asked.

It didn't take an ESPN sports analyst to know the right answer to appease the basketball players jammed into the vehicle, so I named the team their shoes belonged to. I have omitted the team's name from this retelling. Both for their privacy and, as you will find out, to protect the innocent.

"That's what I am talking about!" Bryan said as he managed to offered me a fist bump. I completed the fist bump with an awkward movement of my arm. As it turned out in the shuffle, my seat was as close to the steering wheel as I could afford and leaned straight up, so there was no room for error.

In just under two thousand rides, I have probably only fist bumped only a dozen people.

"So you recognize who are?" Dave asked. I was in a bit of a panic. I'd said they were my favorite team, but I didn't really watch college basketball until March, when the NCAA tournament was played. Even then, I mostly watched the end of the games: not great for facial recognition.

"Of course he recognizes the starting five of his favorite team," Bryan said, winking. I am guessing he saw the blank look on my face, or remembered the fact that I didn't greet them in any special manner.

"Oh man, I can't wait to get back and climb into bed," Markus said. His head was leaned against the window with his eyes shut. As soon as he mentioned it, I too thought of how nice it would be to slip back into bed for a little nap. What I didn't tell the basketball players was that I had spent the day before cleaning on my house, and that morning I had done yard work. I was for sure ready to take a break.

"Yo man, I swear that is all you do," Dave chimed in. I couldn't help but chuckle at this as; it reminded me of a something my younger brother Jacob had said to me as kids.

"Nah, I rain three pointers also," Markus defended. There was a bit of pride in his voice.

"If that were true, we would win all of our games by a bigger margin," Dave said.

"Whatevs, I am killing it out there." Markus waved his hand in the air in what little space he had. It was fun to hear the banter between teammates; it wasn't too different from the same kind of banter I had with co-workers in my office.

"I have to agree with Dave on that one, it is painful watching the game break downs when it comes to you," Bryan said.

This statement really hit home with me. In high school I played on the Varsity football team at Snowflake High School in Arizona. I was not good, and I knew it. The reason was that I had not played organized football until my senior year, and the only reason I was on the Varsity team was because they needed every warm body they could get. After every game we would watch the game breakdown. There is nothing more brutal than a coach pointing out to not just you, but everyone, that you had done something wrong. On the bright side, I had like two plays where the coach actually said, "Good Job."

"Aw man." The guys in the vehicle broke out in laughter.

"Hey! Hey, at least I shoot better than George," Markus said. He made an exaggerated effort to point at George and make sure I knew who he was.

"Come on, man, everyone shoots better than George. Our slick-looking Rideshare driver could probably outshoot George," Bryan said. Again, laughter erupted.

"Why is it you guys always down on me," George said. He was hunched over and his, phone in his hands and frantically texting.

"Man, it is because you are the only guy we know who is texting on the phone with his girl while he is swiping on Tinder," Bryan said. This time I joined the laughter at the comment.

"Whatever," George said as he intently stared at his phone. He looked very much like he was browsing Tinder.

"So, are you a baller?" Bryan asked me. A younger, aged-twenty-one me would have said *for sure, let's go*. However, I was no longer twenty-one. My older body was far from being in any kind of shape for basketball, and it seemed like a lifetime since I had played.

"Back in the day I was alright," I said, remembering times of a younger me. "There were a couple years where I played all the time. I really loved it."

"How long ago was back in the day? You look like you're only in your early thirties," said Bryan.

I smiled. One of the great gifts from my parents were the genes to look younger than I really was. "I wish," I said. "I'm 43 this year. Back in the day was 1996. I served an LDS mission in upstate New York, Utica. Played the projects and watched Syracuse make it to the NCAA finals." I left out that I had played with some super talented individuals, including a couple kids with scholarships to play basketball in college. They taught me a lot. Before that, most of what I knew came from playing basketball at a friend's house in junior high.

"Dang man, that's cool," said Dave. "1996. Was that Carmelo Anthony's team?"

For those unfamiliar with college basketball, this was a very common question. Carmelo played at Syracuse in 2002–03 and won Syracuse its first ever national championship.

"Nah, he was like a decade later; that was John Wallace's team," Dwayne chimed in from the back. He really knew his history when it came to basketball. I wondered if Dwayne was from New York.

"Wait, wait, hold on… do you know Jimmer Fredette?" Bryan asked. Just in case you didn't know Jimmer grew up in Upper State New York: Glens Falls, to be specific. I was super surprised they mentioned the name.

"Come on man, Jimmer isn't that old," Dave said.

"I served near his area, and I played basketball over there. He would have been like seven years old, and to be honest, I don't remember if I met him or not," I said. It was true: as a missionary I played basketball all over the state, and for sure was near where he lived.

Also a true story: on the LDS church court nearest Jimmer, I had the best game of my life. It was on a carpet gym floor, and I went twelve for twelve on a four-on-four game. Though I couldn't seem to miss, and I shot from everywhere, there was one play where, while backpaddling, I tripped over myself and landed flat on my back with everyone cheering for me. So best game and most mortifying game.

"Crazy, yo," Markus said.

"What was really crazy is that a future NFL star played on the team that year," I said.

"Wait. Who?" Bryan asked.

"No other than Donovan McNabb," I said. He had only appeared in five games, but it was really a fun fact that almost no one knew. McNabb would go on to be picked 2nd overall in the NFL draft by the Philadelphia Eagles.

"What?! For reals?" Markus asked.

"Hey Bry, You know what I am looking forward to?" George asked.

"What's that?" Bryan asked.

"Your sister's cooking," George said. This seemed like a really random comment from left field, and everyone visibly wondered where he was going with it.

"Man, what are you talking about?"

"I just came across your sister on "Tinder." George held up his phone. "See?"

Laughter erupted. I tried hard not to laugh with them. I couldn't tell if he was telling the truth or not.

"Dude," Dave said.

"Man, that's not my sister," Bryan said. There was a tone of challenge, but also a little relief.

"It looks just like her?" George asked.

"For sure," Markus said, "but I can tell it isn't her."

"How do you know? You been stalking her on social media?" Bryan asked.

"Nah, we just went out a few days ago," Markus said.

"Whatever, it looks like we we're here," Bryan said. Sure, enough, I was pulling into the parking lot of the drop off point.

I stopped next to the front door of the building. The moment the doors opened, a gush of fresh air rushed in. I hadn't realized how stuffy it had gotten in the vehicle. The crisp air felt a little bit like waking up as it hit my lungs. My whole body felt refreshed.

"Ah, yeah, you guys feel that?" Bryan asked.

"Feel what, your attempt to murder Dwane by making him sit in the back," Marcus asked.

"Nah, it feels like we are going to crush it this season," Bryan said.

I got out to help the guys slowly make their way out of the Dodge Journey, each one offering a fist bump and a "thanks man" on the way out. I slid both of the middle seats forward to help Dwayne escape the very back seat. When he finally made it out of the vehicle, he stretched.

"Oh man, no way am I doing that again," he said. I again started to wonder what vehicles they were used to being picked up in.

"I understand that," I said. I started to reset the seats in the vehicle.

"Hey, thanks again for the ride," Bryan said.

"Anytime!" I said.

That was the first time I managed to fit the starting five of a basketball team into my humble XL. While driving away, I couldn't help but notice that the Journey had really absorbed the cologne. It was going to be a long day after this.

The Fab Five Again

I arrived at an Olympus Burger to pick up my next ride. As neared the entrance, I saw five familiar faces waiting for me. A smile cracked my face as I jumped out to greet the team and prep the Journey. It was a little tortuous that the amazing smell of hamburgers and fries filled the air. It made me long for their quarter-pound Olympus pastrami burger with cheese. And their fries. Olympus Burger had good fries.

I could tell right away that the team recognized me. It helped that I wore the suit and hat; sometimes uniforms are easier to remember than faces. Height, too, made a person recognizable: these were, still, the tallest passengers I knew.

I was nervous that we were going to be stuffing a seven-foot-tall basketball player in the very back again. I noticed they were again wearing expensive high top basketball shoes, but everyone was wearing different ones than before. This time, three of them were tied. The pattern seemed to be random.

"Yo, what's up man," Bryan greeted me. It had been two months.

"Not much. Just driving some rideshare, keeping food on the table for the fam," I replied. I was working towards a slightly different goal during the week of this pickup. I was about to celebrate my anniversary and I wanted to earn some extra money. I was planning a trip down to Las Vegas for a night in a resort hotel, and then a meal at the famed Wynn Breakfast Buffet. (Totally worth it, by the way.)

"You always dress up like this?" Bryan asked, pointing at my suit. I held out my hands and nodded. It wouldn't be until near the end of my rideshare career that I would occasionally wear black slacks, a nice polo, and a riding hat.

"Yes sir, I am here to serve," I said with a grand wave.

"Awesome, good to have you again," Markus said. Everyone offered me a quick fist bump.

"Wait, how big is your family?" Bryan asked.

"Amazing wife and five kids," I replied. As always, I was eager to see what their reply to this would be.

"What?! Five kids?" Markus asked. The expression on everyone's face was priceless. It reminded me of the same face everyone made when Kevin Johnson (6'1) of the Phoenix Suns dunked over Hakeem Olajuwon (7') of the Huston Rockets. If you have never seen this, I recommend checking it out on YouTube.

To me, five kids is not a super large number. I grew up in a family of seven, and so did my wife. My father grew up in a household of fifteen. Still, five was just enough to get a good response

"Yup. Thankfully I have an amazing wife, or else I would be doomed," I said. I thought it was interesting that last time we talked about my time in upper state New York, but I didn't get a chance to mention that that was where I met my wife.

"Man, you can put a whole basketball team on the floor," Bryan said. I laughed. I had heard that before, of course. And it would be true if my kids were into sports. They are mostly into video games, though my oldest daughter ended up doing cheer in high school.

"How old are they?" George asked.

"Three teenagers and two not too far away from that," I said. Saying it out loud always made me feel really, really old.

"So crazy!" Markus said.

"Alright, let's get this show on the road," Bryan said. I realized that this had been the longest I had talked with passengers before loading up and departing, except for the rare occasion that I need to load up luggage.

Unlike the last time, Dwayne had a big smile on his face. Without delay he headed for the front passenger seat. I had to turn away as I started to laugh. Last time he was folded up in the back seat, and that meant someone else was going to be crammed.

"Yeah, let's do this," he said as he climbed in.

"Wait, who is in the back this time?" Markus asked. I was curious to see what was going to happen.

"Don't know, don't care," Dwayne offered as he adjusted the seat. I absolutely loved this comment! The only thing I loved more was the reaction of the other four guys. All of them pointed at each other and then at the back seat.

"I will take the back seat," Dave said.

"Fine by me," Bryan said.

"That is fine by me," Bryan said.

I got into the driver's seat and adjusted the position to help the players fit just a little bit better. It was in that moment It felt like I was driving a Mario Kart: just enough room to safely operate the vehicle, but nothing more. Little did I know that it was training for when I would drive my entire family to California a couple years later. The biggest difference was that the trip to California was about 11 hours.

"This is what I am talking about," Dwayne said pumping his fist into the air out the window.

"Joke's on you, man! How many rides have you paid for just to ensure you get shotgun?" Bryan asked.

"Doesn't matter, totally worth it," Dwayne replied.

"Wait," I said, "you have been paying for the Rideshare rides since the last time I drove you?" My mind was blown at the possibility of how many rides he had covered.

"Nah, just a few," Dwayne said.

The whole vehicle erupted into laughter.

"Yeah right, man, every single rideshare since we were in this one last," Bryan said. It had been two months since I last drove them, so I had guessed he had paid for at least thirty if not more rideshares.

"Like I said, totally worth it," he said. What people might not know is that, as of this book, NCAA players are aren't paid. And their scholarships are not perfect in their coverage. These funds were literally coming out of Dwayne's personal accounts. However, in the not-so-distant future, student athletes will be paid for their contribution to the multi-billion-dollar NCAA industry.

"Yo, what is your craziest story driving Rideshare?" Markus asked. This was a popular question, and to be honest it can be a tough question to answer. It depended on how long I had to tell the story, and who I was telling it to.

"I have a few that fit that description," I said, and went for humor. "There was the Russian girls, the Halloween Passengers, the angry drunk who wanted to fight, and then there is—you guys," I said with a little humor thrown in."

"Wait, you really remember who we are?" Markus asked.

Of course I remembered. I couldn't *forget*. Upbeat conversation, lots of jokes, half a dozen too-tall kids crammed like sardines in a can. At least this time the windows were down, so the cologne wasn't as strong.

"Ain't nobody knows who you are," Dave teased.

"Not if we keep playing the way we have been," Bryan added.

"Your mom knows who I am," Markus tossed back.

The vehicle erupted into laughter. It is almost as if they had not missed a beat from the last ride I gave them.

"Nah, but for reals, do you follow college basketball?" Bryan asked. I was worried that this question would come up, but I couldn't do much about it.

"Not very much," I admitted. "I am more of a fan during March Madness." I had won a couple of NCAA bracket challenges, but beyond that I hadn't watched much.

"Yeah, that is when most of the country cares about college basketball," George chimed in.

"Do you ever pick us to take the tournament?" Bryan followed up.

For a moment, I debated on telling them that I do pick them in the tournament. But I had a hunch that they would see right through it, and I decided to tell them the truth.

"To be honest, I always pick Duke," I said. Coach K was the coach with the most wins in D1 basketball, and statistically he was a pretty safe choice.

The air was filled with mocking painful noises.

"I thought you were a fan of ours," Bryan said.

"For sure support you guys, and will be routing for you," I said, "If it helps, I hope you prove me wrong. I always pick you for one or two rounds."

"Yeah, but Coach K is a solid choice," Bryan said.

"This is our year," Dave said.

"Again, not if we keep playing the way we have been," Bryan said.

"Yeah, of course you get to cover Zion," Dwayne said. He was referencing Duke's 6'7 player Zion Williamson, who went on to be drafted first round, first pick by the New Orleans Pelicans.

"I will gladly take him on when we get there," Bryan said.

"Oh man, someone needs to take George's phone away," Markus said.

"Man leave me alone," George said. His head was buried in the screen.

"Is he hitting up Tinder again?" Bryan asked.

"Maybe we should tell coach," Markus replied. This comment seemed to strike home; George looked up and paid attention.

"Ok, ok, I am putting it away, just take it easy," George said. He slid the phone into a pocket. The reaction caused me to wonder. Too many dates? Too many late nights? Too many parties? Or too many complaints?

"I don't get it. You are with a smoking hot girl already, what are you doing?" Dave asked.

"He knows she is going to realize that he doesn't have a future in basketball and leave him," Dwayne said. "She's just hanging in there, just in case he gets lucky."

"Whatever, whatever," George waved his hand.

It was at that point I pulled up to the drop off point, which happened to be the exact same place as last time. I was disappointed that the ride was short this time. I enjoyed the fun banter.

"Whatever, whatever," George waved his hand.

It was at that point I pulled up to the drop off point, which happened to be the exact same place as last time. I was disappointed that the ride was short this time. I enjoyed the fun banter.

"Aw, man, I wanted to hear about the Russian girls," Dave said.

"Maybe next time," I said.

"Yo, you should write that into a book or something!" George said. (Sound advice that, thankfully, I had already started working on.)

"Why? You wouldn't be able to read it," Bryan said.

"I can read just fine. I just finished the Grapes of Wrath," George said.

"Then why does it seem like you can't read the plays," Bryan shot back.

Everyone erupted in laughter.

I got out to help extract the team from the vehicle; like before, each gave me a fist bump on their way out. As I drove away, I could see them laughing and chiding each other. I wish I could tell you that I picked them up again and I got to tell them the Russian story, but I never saw any of the guys ever again.

Somewhere in the back of my mind, I wonder if Dwayne is still paying for rideshare rides so he can pick the seat he ends up in. It was good to get to meet them and get a little reacquainted. During my years of driving, I only ever had four repeat passenger requests. This was one of my favorite ones.

Ode to Scott

Once upon a time there was a potential Rideshare passenger
    named Scott,
he decided to go somewhere and requested a ride or so he
    thought.

He activated the app which alerted the driver (me) of the ride,
8 minutes away the drivers finger to accept did slide.

Thinking 8 minutes was too long Scott canceled the request,
but reconsidered a few minutes later recreating the behest.

Now 12 minutes away the driver (me) again tried,
but Scott quickly denied.

Rejected further the driver resumed course away,
but Scott was determined to change his mind anyway.

One last time Scott activated the Rideshare request,
and this time the driver (me) was 17 minutes away and accepted
    the quest.

To no one's surprise Scott did rescind the order once again,
causing the driver to wonder what was Scott's constraint.

May Scott someday decide to finally complete a Rideshare ride.
    Someday.

Pouty Paula

This is the story of Paula who was exceptionally pouty,
who I picked up after dropping off people who were rowdy.
The name listed on the app was Heather,
who called and explained she needed her daughter home
despite the snowy weather.

Understanding the concerned and desperate mother,
I mentally switched to think like a big brother.
Paula reached the car and quickly climbed in:
"You have probably already talked with my mother and heard
her spin."

"Yes, and I will get you up Parley's Canyon safe."
"I am 26 years old, you know, and her control is starting to
chafe."
"She really sounded extremely worried."
Paula just answered by staring at the snow that flurried.

As we headed up the canyon I tried to make small talk,
but all that she would do in reply was balk.
Her arms folded firm and her eye fixed out the window,
Thoughts wandering off into limbo.

At the end of the forty-five-minute trip,

she glanced over at me with a look like she could flip.

"You didn't have to pick me up, you know."

she huffed and dragged her backpack in tow.

I watched her walk up to the house,

I started to drive away quiet as a mouse.

I am not sure how that family dynamic works,

But driving pouty Paula ended up having its perks.

I got a very large tip from her much-worried mother,

and got to see she made it safe, satisfying that mentality of brother.

I do always wonder if Paula didn't want to go home,

why get into a Rideshare ride instead of continuing to roam.

People are so fascinating without a doubt,

but taking care of each other is what life is all about.

Stephen The Astrophysicist

I was looking for a passenger early one Saturday afternoon,
when passing by the airport I heard the passenger Rideshare tune.
As I had done hundreds of times before,
I drove to the terminal to see what was in store.

As I pulled up Stephen asked, "Are you okay going to Logan?"
"For sure, I will get you there safe" I chanted my slogan.
As we headed to the destination up North,
I asked what to Utah had brought him forth.

"An annual conference of sorts."
"Oh, which one would happen so far from the airport?"
"It's the Characterization and Radiometric Calibration for Remote
    Sensing."
"It's an astronomical conference referred to CALCON when
    condensing."

"Wow, sounds pretty awesome to me" I said impressed.
"It can be, but it is pretty technical," he stressed.
I wondered, "How did you end up getting into astronomy?"
"Oh, I would look up as a kid and imagine space with all of its
    autonomy."

After the hour-and-twenty-minute trip came to an end,
Stephen grabbed his bags and headed into the hotel.
"Thanks for choosing Rideshare and happy star gazing," I yell.
With long pause I look at the route back to Salt Lake,
wishing for a fare all the way back I ache.

I always remember Stephen my first astrophysicist and longest
    ride,
as well as the conference CALCON simplified.

Do you come here often?

Once I am underway with a passenger, the first thing I like to do is thank them for using rideshare. Then I ask them if they use it often. This helps me gauge their expectations, and is my first peek into what sort of experience I should craft. In this regard, there are three types: those who use rideshare all the time, those who have used it here and there only, and those who are brand new to the service.

It surprised me the number of people who got rid of their cars and rely entirely on rideshare. One of my repeat passengers was like this. Her name was Melody; she worked for two different fast food chains and commuted between them. She explained that rideshare was easier than owning her own vehicle. She wasn't plagued by refilling the gas tank, oil changes, registration, insurance, parking, or vehicle repair.

At the time, she'd purchased a monthly pass for the rideshare company that gave her a flat rate for every trip. That pass has since been discontinued. I often wonder if it is still affordable for her to use rideshare all the time.

Those who use rideshare only occasionally tend to be snobbish about it. They like to remind me that they know and understand All Things. These people are the most comfortable ignoring me while they make phone calls or read through their email; they can be harder to engage in conversation.

I once drove a TV producer who had headed a handful of popular shows. I picked him and his family up from the airport, and was taking them to pick up their rental vehicle. He explained that typically they rented a car from the airport, but that it was significantly less expensive to rent it from the place I was taking them. He wasn't interested in making much conversation, but his wife was friendly.

When we reached our destination, it was not the rental place he had intended. Flustered, he began cycling through his emails and searching for answers. We confirmed the address several times.

I suggested that we try driving down the road to see if we could spot the place, as it probably wasn't far away. The passenger insisted that we not, because it would charge him more. Realistically it would have cost an additional $0.25 for the distance we were looking at. He found the number and called to find out it was indeed just a half mile down the road, and he had to pay the extra $0.25 anyways.

People who use the service for the first time or not very often are really fun to talk to. They are outside their comfort zone.

Conversation helps them relax and enjoy the ride. These passengers often just gaze out the window or ask questions about how ridesharing works.

There was one passenger, Steven, who was super nervous during his very first ride. He looked out the window and clasped his hands together between his knees. When I asked a question, his voice was shaky and uncertain. After a few questions, I was able to get a dialogue going and he told me how much he really enjoyed the experience.

Steven: "Are you sure you know where we're going?"

Me: "Yes sir, I have it on the app right here."

Steven: "…"

Me: "Have you used ridesharing before?"

Steven: "…"

Me: "No worries, I have been doing this for a minute. I will get you there safely."

Steven: "Thank…. Thank You."

Me: "Thank you for using rideshare, by the way."

Steven: "You're welcome. Sorry, I am just kind of nervous."

Me: "I couldn't tell."

Steven: "Really?"

Me: "Yeah, nothing to worry about. Are we headed someplace important?"

Steven: "Yeah, I am going to go propose to my girlfriend."

Me: "…"

Sometimes I am surprised by the answer to the question: have you used rideshare before? I have had people who had bad experiences previously, but who were giving rideshare another chance. There were those who just didn't like it but had to use it under their specific circumstances. I have had some who told me they were rideshare drivers themselves. Then, there were the bizarre passengers who took it as their cue to lecture me about how the government tracked people through things like rideshare apps.

One ride was particularly embarrassing, but not for the passenger. The embarrassed person was me. I didn't realize my passenger was a repeat customer. During our first ride, she had enjoyed the conversation and felt like we'd made a good connection as people. She even gave me a generous tip for it. On our second ride, I launched into my typical opening questions. She asked if I remembered her. To be honest, I absolutely didn't. The silence grew awkward very quickly after that.

Needless to say, there was no tip that time.

Saltair Stormy Rave

The first ride I gave to the Great Saltair facility was more interesting than I could have predicted. I was called to downtown Salt Lake to a prominent hotel. When I arrived, the pickup point was crowded with several dozen people. They were in a wide variety of clothing styles; I would probably describe them as Rocky Horror Picture show meets High School Musical.

It only took a moment for my six passengers to emerge from the gathering. I jumped out of the vehicle to help them in.

For years, I had heard about concerts out at Saltair, but had never been there in person. (I attended a Billie Eilish concert there with two of my daughters a year later.) Having at one point lived out in Tooele, Utah while working in Salt Lake City, I *had* driven past the most recent iteration of the facility many times.

Fun fact: Saltair was first built in 1893 as a resort on the Great Salt Lake. It was through a series of several fires and rebuilds that we ended up with the current version, built in 1981. The recent version was constructed from a salvaged aircraft hangar from Hill Air Force Base, and though initially plagued with flooding, it is currently nowhere near the water.

"Heather?" I asked.

"Jared?" she asked. We both nodded, and I started opening the doors to the Journey and slid the middle seat forward. Her boisterous group of very happy people started filling the vehicle.

"Have you taken many groups out to Saltair today?" Heather asked.

"You are the first," I said. It was an interesting question, in that I had no idea what Saltair might be hosting that would cause me to drive so many people there.

"Oh, you are in for a treat the next couple of days," Heather said.

"Really? What's going on?" I asked.

"There's a huge rave going on out there. It's going to be so much fun!" she said.

"Awesome," I said. I had friends who had been to raves; I wondered what they actually looked like. Like many people, I have only seen them in movies and on TV shows.

As I pulled away from the hotel, the passengers all started clapping and whooping. They were asking each other who they wanted to see at the rave when I entered the freeway. In the distance, dark gray storm clouds slunk in from the West.

The closer we got to Saltair, the more menacing the storm became. Strong gusts of wind pushed the Journey back and forth on the road. Lightning started to strike the top of the stack at the Rio Tinto Kennecott Smelter plant.

"That doesn't look good," I mentioned. It didn't seem like it was going to be a light rainstorm, but a full-blown thunderstorm.

"No, it doesn't," Heather agreed.

"Oh no," Stephen said.

"What? What happened?" Heather asked.

"The outdoor stage is temporarily closed due to high winds," he said. At that moment a huge gust of wind pushed against the Journey. I was able to correct, but everyone felt it. At the speeds I was traveling, I was getting a little nervous; I started to slow down.

"Aw man," the passengers let out a collective groan of disappointment.

"That's alright, the winds will calm down. Plus, it's about who is on the main stage inside," Heather said. I wondered if she had been to events out at Saltair previously, because to me it didn't look like there was going to be a calm in the storm any time soon.

"Good point," Steve said.

"Hey, did I mention that I love your hat?" Heather said to me.

"Thank you! I got it at Salt Lake FanX," I said. It is true that I got the hat from FanX, but it was inspired by a situation where I was on a panel with other amazing guests. When the panel concluded I walked down and started talking with people that had been in the audience; no one seemed to realize that I had been on the panel. My wife and I devised a plan to level up my branding: thus, the suit and fedora was a Thing. It continues to pay dividends today.

"Awesome. Can I take a picture wearing your hat," she asked. It was the first time someone had asked to wear it, but it wouldn't be the last. I should probably be worried about catching something, but I've never really thought about it. I *have* thought about starting an Instagram just for the hat.

"Sure," I said. I handed the dark grey fedora to her. She quickly put it on and snapped a selfie.

"Oh! That looks nice on you," Steve said. Everyone who has tried that hat on ends up loving the hat. One ride offered to buy it from me for $100. I almost sold it to them.

"Heck yeah, you totally rock that!" another passenger agreed.

"I know, I think I totally dig it," Heather said. She handed the hat back.

We got close to the Saltair exit and were immediately greeted by a long line of cars waiting to drop people off or park. Though there was a series of traffic signs warning of long lines, I was caught off guard by the length of the line. I would learn, months later, that the lack of real infrastructure at Saltair would always hold it back from its real potential.

"Should we walk from here?" Heather asked the collective group. Up ahead we could see people getting out of their rides and starting to walk towards the entrance. The entrance was still nearly two miles away.

"Nah, it will only take us a few more minutes before get up there. And we're going to be on our feet the whole night," Stephen said. This statement would really hit home for me when I attended the Billie Eilish concert a year later. There was pretty much no place to sit in the venue, and I ended up standing for hours.

"Good call," Heather said.

"Do you go to many of these concerts?" I asked. The song "Rock n' roll lifestyle" by Cake ran through my mind.

"Do we? Hah, Steve how many have we been to this year?" Heather asked.

"Oh, let see, there were the two in Vegas, then Phoenix, Los Angeles, San Diego, Seattle, Portland, and now here," Stephen said. "Of course, we still have a few more left to go this year."

"That sounds awesome. Do you do this every year?" I asked. I attempted to do the mental math to figure out what that would cost. Then I wondered what kind of jobs these people had.

"So far," Heather replied.

Just as it seemed as though my passengers were going to decide to walk the remainder of the way, the large group of people who had just passed were knocked over by the wind. The dozen bodies scattered across the ground and scrambled to get back to their feet. This revealed far more of the scantily clad individuals than anyone ever wanted to see. Instantly, an unspoken decision was made by the passengers to wait until they were at the drop off point.

"That storm is looking worse," I said as a series of three lighting strikes hit the top of the Kennecott smelter stack off in the distance. Of the many times I had passed the stack during a storm, I had never seen it struck once. (The stack was built in 1974 and stands 1,215 feet tall. So in reality, it shouldn't have been that surprising that it was getting hit.)

Another large group of attendees passed by the vehicle while we waited in line. The choice of clothing was by far the riskiest I had seen to that point. The fabric either didn't cover the necessary parts of the human anatomy to keep someone from being labeled naked, or it covered it but was super sheer.

Most of the attendees wore clothing that was perfectly good. None of it was my personal style *or* color; I felt the stirrings of discomfort.

"Yeah, but at least we should be safe inside," Heather said. "Stephen, any updates on the concerts?"

"Nope, looks like everything is still on schedule," he said.

"Oh good," everyone sighed with relief.

"Can we get a picture with you, Mr. Rideshare driver?" One of the people in the back asked. They already had one of the hat, so why not one that has me *and* the hat?

"Oh, good idea," Heather said. She pulled out her phone and set it to take a selfie.

"You're cool with this, right?" she asked.

"Yeah," I said. Just as I answered, the phone snapped the picture.

"When we are at the drop off point, would you have time for a lay?" a girl in the back asked.

I was shocked. I wondered what she was thinking. In all honesty, I thought I was being propositioned.

"Um, I don't think so, I am married," I said. I glanced into the rear-view mirror.

The whole vehicle erupted into laughter. I glanced around to see if I could figure out the joke.

"No silly, not lay, I mean lei as in we give you a Hawaiian flower lei," she said.

Oh. I had genuinely misunderstood; but I was glad, too, to have been wrong.

"Oh, yes, that would be cool," I said.

Finally, after another ten minutes and hundreds of people walking past getting blown over by the wind, we pulled up to the designated drop zone. I got out to help the group out of the Journey. The strong wind caused everyone to lean forward a little as they headed for the building.

"Good luck! Enjoy the concert," I said.

"You too, be safe," Heather shouted back.

I got back into the Journey just in time for another pick up to ping me out somewhere near the airport. Sure enough, it was another group heading to Saltair.

Stormy Rave (part 2)

As I left the concert venue of Saltair, I could see sideways rain and black ominous storm clouds chasing me East down the I–80. The wind pushed us all around on the highway; I worried about staying on the road. I worried more about the large cargo trucks I passed as they swayed along the route. I wondered if the group I had just dropped off would get to enjoy their concert.

The pickup point for this next group was at a group of micro hotels west of the airport. I pulled up to a brand-new building; the group waiting for me were dressed, best as I can describe, in skimpy goth. The app quickly confirmed that they were headed to Saltair.

"Are you Jared?" Trent asked after opening the passenger door.

"Yes sir," I responded. "Trent?"

"Yup!" he confirmed.

I jumped out to help the group get situated. In the process, the strong winds nearly knocked me over. They did push two people to fall against the vehicle. The passengers were cheering and clapping as they loaded into the Journey.

"That storm coming in is causing the venue issues, just so you know," I mentioned to the group. From how fast the storm was pushing in, I suspected that Saltair was now engulfed by the worst of it.

"What kind of issues?" Trent asked.

I hated being the bearer of bad news, but I knew they would want to know. "They have closed the outdoor stage due to wind, and, by now, also wind and lightning."

"As long as the indoor stuff is still running, then we are all good," he replied.

"As far as I know," I replied.

"Yeah!" the passengers cheered.

As we merged onto the highway, the conversation was lively and rife with anticipation. Then, a passenger from the back seat called out:

"Hey! I love the hat, it would go perfect with my outfit for this," the passenger said. I glanced back to see. They were in a black leather-looking jacket with a white mesh undershirt, and short black cutoffs.

"That is the best part: it pretty much goes with any outfit," I said with a laugh.

"How much you want for it?" they asked.

"Unfortunately, I can't sell it; it has been on too many adventures with me," I said.

"I totally understand. You do your thing; I respect that," they said.

This time as I headed for Saltair, the line of cars at exit was miles long, far out of sight of the main building. I couldn't even see the traffic signs warning of long wait times that I had seen earlier that day. Slowly, we puttered forward. We were still in the line when the heavy rainstorm unleased its awesome fury. Water blanketed the windows, making it near impossible to see.

"Oh man, all this rain is making me need to pee," one of the male passengers said.

One fact about the stretch of I–80 that leads to Saltair: there are no trees, and the bushes are very thin and sparse. In other words, no chance of privacy if someone were desperate.

"Why did you say that; I need to go now too," a female passenger said.

"Are you kidding me right now? I told you to go before we left," Trent said. It sounded like the kind of thing I'd heard on family road trips growing up.

"I did, but I think those last few drinks are just running through me," the male passenger said.

"Well, what is your plan? You can't pee in here," Trent said. I couldn't agree more. Thankfully, no one had ever attempted to before.

"I will go out in the rain," the male passenger said.

"Me too," the female passenger said.

The only advantage they had was that we were not going anywhere anytime soon. Though the drop off had been on the small side, it was efficient in getting people in and out. I wasn't quite sure what the holdup was, unless there was an accident someplace.

"Oh, well, this is going to be rich," Trent said. "Go for it."

The two people jumped out of the vehicle and dashed to the tiny little bushes nearby, which concealed nothing from anyone, as the rain had lightened just in time. A couple of minutes later the two came dashing back into the car. In retrospect, I think an attempt right next to the vehicle would have provided more privacy.

"Do you feel better?" Trent asked.

"Well, yes," they both said.

"Ugh, we are still like two miles away, and we are moving so slow," another passenger complained. Actually, we were still three and a half miles out, but I wasn't about to correct them.

"And what will you be doing about that?' Trent asked. His sarcastic tone left little room to read between the lines. The frustration of waiting in a line, plus the weather, plus the awkward public display left him on edge.

"I think I am going to walk. It will be so much faster, plus I can vape," the passenger said. If it weren't for the rain, I would have agreed. (To the walking, and the vaping outside.) After all, the rain was worse than the wind, which had thankfully passed.

"If you go, I will go with you," another passenger said.

"Go for it. Go walk in the rain; we will see you up there," Trent said.

"Alright," the passenger said. The two people got out and started walking towards the destination. They weren't alone: there were dozens of reluctant ravers on foot heading towards the destination in the rain.

"Hey, how did you know the outdoor stage was closed when you picked us up?" one of the remaining passengers asked.

"The last group I took told me. I suspect they had an app or twitter or something," I replied.

"Cool," they said.

Trent turned to me and hesitated before asking, "Was it this slow for your last ride out here?"

I could tell that he knew the answer but was hoping for a different one. It pained me a little to break it to him.

"Not even close. It was slow, but the line was pretty short compared to this," I said.

"Ugh, bad news," a passenger in the back said. The contempt and disappointment were heavy in his voice.

"What's that?" Trent asked.

"They just posted that they are not letting anyone in the building, and no one is playing on any stage right now," the passenger said.

"Does it say why?" he asked.

"Yeah, weather conditions," the passenger said.

"What? Weather conditions? How is that affecting the main stage inside?" another passenger said.

"We paid for these super VIP passes, so they better let us in the door or I am going to freak out on them," Trent said. I could tell he wanted to use much stronger language, but he glanced at me halfway through his reply. The suit and hat had a tendency of doing that sort of thing. I can't tell you how many swearwords, inappropriate statements, phrases, and gestures the suit had prevented. It was like a non-verbal request for a higher standard.

Just then the line of cars started moving at a good rate, and it wasn't long before we were past the two people who were walking. Trent made it a point to wave at them through the window.

"Look, now we are past them, and they are all wet," Trent said.

"Brilliant," a passenger said laughing.

"Well, if we get out and walk, we will just have to wait for them to open the doors. We might as well wait in the Rideshare ride," Trent said. I nodded.

"I am with you on that," a passenger said.

"Hey, do you have an aux cord? Can we play our tunes while we wait in line?" Trent asked. This was a really common request from passengers, especially groups. Tragically the only cord I had that fed into the audio system was the same one I used to charge my iPhone, so Android users were out of luck.

"Sure thing," I said. I handed him the cord. After plugging it in, he selected a song and I turned up the radio. Now just a mile out from Saltair, we were nearly a half mile past the two people who had elected to walk. The music was thumping and everyone in the car was happily waving their hands all about. After a few songs, we were surprised to hear a knock on the rear passenger window.

"Hey, so, can we get back in?" The two passengers who had been walking asked.

"It's up to the rideshare driver," Trent said. I laughed at the prospect of denying them entry, after all they were wet from the rain and all, but I am not a mean person.

"Sure, let them back in," I said.

Everyone laughed as they rejoined the group. Song after song played, until we finally got to the top of the ramp. With the music in place, there wasn't any more conversation, but the music offered a different kind of connection. There were songs that I had never heard before, some that sounded strange to me, and several that were straight off my own playlist. At this point the rain was just a trickle. Droves of people were now walking towards the main building. Though we weren't to the drop off site, we were within sight of it.

"Okay, I think this is the end of the ride for us here," Trent said.

"Sounds good! Good luck getting in, and enjoy the show," I said.

"Thanks," Trent said.

I don't know if Trent and his friends ended up in the venue or getting to see anything that night. It wasn't long after I got on the highway to Salt Lake that I was called back to Saltair to pick people up. I made the run several times that night. Some had made it into the venue, some didn't.

The next day the weather was nice, and I returned to make several runs to and from Saltair all day. I hoped to catch a glimpse of Trent or Heather and their groups, but never did. I hope they enjoyed themselves.

Soda Jerk

One weekday evening, I had just finished up a quick board meeting with one of the non-profits I worked with. I got a call to pick up a person from a Maverik convenience store. It only took me a couple of minutes to arrive at the pickup spot. Outside there was only one guy wearing a black puffer jacket, blue jeans, and a Chicago Cubs beanie. In his right hand was a foam 64 oz big drink.

As soon as I reported my arrival through the app, the lone figure approached the vehicle. I got out to go open the door for him.

"Donald?" I asked.

"Yeah, that's me," he said. "Hey look, I don't need any extra BS service. I can get my own door; let's just get going."

His comment was odd and abrasive, but he had a big smile and laughed immediately after saying it. I thought I could smell just a touch of alcohol on his breath, but nothing led me to believe he was outright drunk.

"Okay," I said. I promptly walked back and slid into the driver seat. "It looks like we are headed just a few blocks away."

It wasn't unusual to take people just around the corner for a quick trip. Often times it was to and from a convenience or state liquor store.

"Yup," he said.

I noticed that he was looking at his phone and tipping his cup forward quite a bit. Even though it had a lid, I wanted to be cautious. "There is a cup holder in the center of that seat if you would like."

"Oh." He pulled down the armrest and placed the foam big drink into the cup holder.

"Thank you for choosing rideshare," I said. I shifted the Journey into gear and headed out of the parking lot.

"Yeah, no problem. It's funny; I actually own six different companies. Each makes about ten million dollars a year in profit," he said. I could tell he was leaning forward quite a bit from the swishing sound of his puffer jacket and sound of his voice.

"That is cool; what kind of businesses are they?" I asked. I love being curious, especially when people are offering good tidbits.

"You know, a little of this and a little of that," he replied. It wasn't a surprising answer; people tend to become a little protective when they realize they said more than they should.

I wasn't quite sure how to reply to that, so I simply said, "Awesome."

"I respect the side hustle though. I mean, it takes an entrepreneurial spirt. That is how I made my first million dollars," he said as he leaned back against his seat. His bragging was only a little interesting, but he wanted to talk, and I knew that ending the conversation tended to irritate people like this.

I offered the most appeasing and enthusiastic thing I could think of: "Wow."

"You think that is impressive, I have houses all over the world." He waved his arms about in the back seat like I could see them.

"That is really impressive. Are you based in Salt Lake or just visiting?" I was trying to figure out this person. There was a little hint of an accent, but I couldn't quite place it.

"I grew up here, so I have a thing for this place." He finished his sentence with a boisterous laugh.

"At least you get to travel often, it sounds like," I said.

"What does that mean?" he asked. The tone got serious fast.

"It's just with houses all over the world and stuff." I attempted to deescalate the situation.

"Yeah, but I never get to see them. Just my family; they are all jealous of me. They all want to be me," he said. "But I am the responsible one who has to keep the lights on. You know what I mean, right?"

At this point I wasn't sure what to think, so I responded, "Sure."

"Hum," he said.

I turned into an older neighborhood, where there was a sense of a pride on clean lines in the lawn, well curated flowers, and really well-kept façades. The app directed me to a smaller house near the end of the street. It had not aged well and seemed to be in a state of disrepair. Though I had known wealthy people who lived in modest accommodations, this was a whole other level. I wondered if we had arrived at the correct address.

"Is this good?" I asked.

"Yes," he said.

He opened the door, and as he started to pull his cup out of the holder, he immediately put it back in. I looked back to see what was going on.

"Is everything alright?" I asked.

"Oh, man, it looks like my straw somehow punctured the bottom of the cup and it's leaked into the cup holder."

"Yikes." I didn't want to overreact at the news until I could see the damage for myself.

I got out of the car and walked around, just in time to see him yank the cup from the cup holder, spilling soda on the floor and seat. The cup holder was completely filled with soda. I was fortunate that the inside of the cupholder was a solid plastic.

"No worries, man, I will tip you generous to clean that up," he said waving at the mess.

There wasn't much I could do at the moment, so I planned getting back to the gas station just around the corner. I offered a quick, "Okay."

"Well, good luck with that." He quickly entered the house.

I opened the floor compartment and pulled out some paper towels to do damage control. That was when I realized his soda was spiked with alcohol. The sweet and sour sent was unmistakable. Realizing that it was going to take more effort and resources than I had on hand, I closed the door and got back into the Journey. As I had planned, I drove down to the nearest gas station, and reassessed. After taking several pictures, I attacked with Febreze, disinfectant wipes, and water. With how saturated everything was, I wasn't going to be able to take on any more passengers for the night at least.

Defeated, I got back into the Journey. A short time later, the app reported that the rider gave me three starts and a three-dollar tip. Frustrated at the loss of income and the poor review, I pulled over. I submitted one of only a handful of complaints against a rider I have ever made. As required, I had to submit photo evidence. By the time I reached home for the evening, the report had come back; the rideshare company issued me a one-hundred-dollar payout for the incident.

While driving for rideshare companies, I had passengers of just about every imaginable type. I have driven billionaires and millionaires typically because rideshare companies are cheaper than car services. During those rides, they never bragged about being rich; they would just mention things that implied that they were. Their drop off points typically confirmed any suspicions.

Interesting side note: one of the wealthiest people I ever met drove a Geo Metro, lived in a cramped basement apartment, and shoveled walkways in the winter. There are many who feel like they need to peacock, so people will be impressed by them.

The soda jerk could sure talk the talk, but for a peacock, he had no idea how to walk.

Carl the past Coworker: Take One

I wasn't surprised when I pulled up to a quaint little bar,
after 1,300 rides to find an acquaintance climbing into my car.
"Hey man, it is so good to see you."
I tipped my fedora and, "good to see you too."

"Do you mind if I stop by my car to get my bottle of gin."
"Sure thing, you're the boss; better grab it before we begin."
After a moment Carl return with bottle in hand,
he said, "let's escape this forsaken wonderland."

As we drove, he told me the directions,
the same ones he thought Siri should have had in its map's
    collections.
"You know what is wrong with the world today?"
He continued, "those gosh darn Bears have won too many,
    leaving me no leeway."

I replied, "oh, yeah, and now you owe dinner to another former
    co-worker."
"Yup, and to none other than that crazy subverter."
I added, "Remember the days we all sat round the ol' office,
talking of how our lives were good but too cautious."

He said, "how things change in such a short period of time,
the little time we hang together now is something of a crime."
He asked, "can I take a swig of your Mountain Dew?"
Before I could answer he was guzzling I think more than he knew.

"Well you can keep that," I said with restraint.
"Oh no, I just wanted a sip it is all yours," feeling like he had
    constraint.

In short order we reached the final destination,
He offered me a considerable tip for the soda confiscation.

It was so good to see my dear old friend,
I could only hope that it would become a regular trend.
I wouldn't give up my friends or family for anything,
In this world and the next, to me they mean everything.

Carl the past Coworker: Round Two

Early in the morning I was surprised to be summoned to a
    familiar home,
Of my good friend who works on studying the human genome.
Funny that I had just seen him just the night before;
I wondered what funny stories this trip was going to have in store.

Carl climbed in with his child in the back seat,
He asked to head to the nearest gas station to grab a treat.
I gladly acquiesced his simple typical passenger request,
He generously snagged me a large bag of beef jerky,
And handed a cup of hot chocolate to his cute little turkey.

"Thank you so much for getting me home late last night;
I know that most of the drinkers at my table were pretty light."
"No problem, I am always more than happy to give you a ride,
plus there weren't too many secrets that you would have to
    confide."

"Good thing you know exactly where my car is hopefully still at;
we are on a time table to get this little one to pottery class, and
    stat."
"Sounds like a whole lot of pottery fun."
"Well it is so much better than the typical humdrum."

"Just out of sheer curiosity:
Is there much difference today over last night's personality?"
"I would say you are two separate men,
but nothing I wouldn't happily drive again."

As we arrived to the parking lot of the quaint little bar,
Carl let out a sigh of relief to see his car.

"I hope to catch you another time!"
"Give me a call, summer, spring, and even wintertime."

Again, I parted with my good ol' Craig,
Whom without a doubt is a very good egg.
I never mind driving everyone to where they need to go,
Drunk or sober, it is basic human kindness on show.

Breaking through the Ice

Aside from how often a passenger uses rideshare, there is another set of markers for passenger behavior. Namely: how they respond to my efforts to break the ice. Sometimes more work is needed to get them to engage; sometimes less.

The first of these are people who are working intently on their phone or scrolling through social media. The second are people eager to chat. The third are outliers: people who are tired and want to sleep, people with language barriers, people already talking to someone on the phone. The fourth: large groups. Most large groups want music. Some want to control the music themselves. If it is a family with younger kids, I keep the music down.

For those who are working on their phones, I turn the music up to just a little past background noise. The idea plays on psychology. They are so focused on their phone that they initially don't notice. When a new song starts, it acts as a disruptive influence. The transition from the moment of silence between songs allows their brain to multitask a little more. The music on the verge of too loud breaks their chain of thought when the next song starts. More often than not, their faces go puzzled, and they look up and out the window. When that happens, I jump in with an icebreaker.

It's not a perfect science, and it doesn't work 100% of the time. But it does work about 95% of the time. I want to say that only a handful of people stayed on their devices regardless.

My most popular go-to is, "What kind of work do you do?" This uses a bit of clever neuroscience. According to an article in the Scientific American website, 60% of people's favorite topic is their own thoughts and experiences.[i] It actually jumps up to 80% when the medium is social media. While driving passengers, I have found in my own non-scientific study that closer to 90% of people like to talk about themselves. So, this icebreaker is incredibly effective. My second go-to is, "Are you from around here?" This is replaced with, "Are you just visiting or coming home," if I am picking someone up from the airport.

It helps that I am genuinely interested in what people are saying, so I am using my active listening while driving. The only time I don't is during severe weather, heavy traffic, or nearing a destination in a busy area of the city.

The icebreaker is only part one of an effective strategy. A good icebreaker will get you a response, but it is the follow-up questions that really fuel a conversation. Things that encourage the passenger to keep going. Questions like, "wow, that sounds fascinating, what is that like?" Or, "Just curious, how did you end up in that industry?" From there, the conversation just flows.

Some people will try to answer with one-word answers for everything. I learned pretty quickly that if I am to keep the conversation going, I have to turn that answer into an open-ended question. For instance, I had one passenger that said he was an IRS tax auditor. I followed up with, "What is that like?"

To which he answered, "Good."

I asked, "What kind of training is required for something like a tax auditor?"

The man paused. I honestly don't think he had been asked that question with real interest. This time, he opened up about what schooling he had gone through, and the various certifications he'd earned. I mentioned that he would have gotten along with my dad, who was a CPA. Next thing I know, we were talking about what kinds of public cases he was working on. Which was absolutely fascinating, but left out of this book because I am not positive they should have been going into as much detail as they did.

I was pretty fortunate in that the music strategy had never backfired on me. The icebreaking, on the other hand, backfired once. I tried to engage with a passenger who started to not only spout various alien and government conspiracies, but by the end of the ride accused me of being in on it. It went something like this.

Me: "How are you doing today?"

Passenger: "I really don't know how I should respond to that. Fine, I guess."

Me: "Are you from Utah?"

Passenger: "Sometimes."

Me: "Cool."

Passenger: "Nah, man, it is hot."

Me: "True, it is in the 90's out there."

Passenger: "What? The 90's is when Perkins told us the about fluoride, and we were not listening."

Me: "…"

Passenger: "They are all in on it, you know? The aliens and the historians."

Me: "Oh?"

Passenger: "Wait, wait, are you one of them? Did they plant you here for me? Just let me off at this gas station."

Here is the most interesting part: even though the dialogue seems crazy, the passenger was calm and only mildly emotional in their responses.

Every once in a while, there is an obvious question that begs to be asked because of situation, circumstance or other variable. One time, I was pretty certain I was driving a spy or murderer.

Okay, so both of those are real stretches. But, in the moment, they were actual thoughts in my mind.

Imagine what you would be thinking if this happened to you:

I arrived at the pickup zone and found myself in a parking lot with just one other vehicle, an all-black SUV with super dark tinted windows. The app showed that my passenger was moving really fast down the street. Two different rideshare vehicles pulled up and dropped off two people, a man and a woman. The two walked over to the SUV, opened the trunk, and pulled out some luggage. Then they locked the SUV and got into my vehicle. I tried to ask questions, but they were not talkative at all and they were headed to the international part of the Salt Lake Airport. Which, at the time, Salt Lake only had flights to Mexico from the international part of the airport. To top it off, they didn't tip.

So maybe I was a little jaded after that. But. It was suspicious.

When I could get people to engage in conversation, it increased the chances of getting a tip. However, there were some odd consistencies when it comes to that aspect of driving. Most wealthy people either did not tip, or they tipped very little. One time I dropped of a couple at a ski resort and the guy literally tipped me two quarters. Middle class and poorer people were the most generous with tips.

Here is an interesting thing to think about: from my own pool of passengers, 1 out of 15 wealthy people tipped, while 8–10 middle class and poorer people left tips. However, the 1 wealthy person who tipped would sometimes equal more than the 8 combined tips from the other group. Also, drunk people would tip most often, and more generously, than sober people.

So I worked hard, and assumed everyone had the potential to tip.

Regardless of the ride, I always deployed the various strategies with music and icebreaking question. The conversations were mostly rewarding. Honestly, people are far more interesting than they think they are. (I told them this, frequently, and they dismissed it more often than not. It was unfortunate.)

The Tallahassee Six

The sun had retired hours before I got the notification to pick up a large group of people in Salt Lake. As I pulled up to the modest restaurant indicated on the map, I flipped on my hazards. The road didn't have a shoulder to use. The group that approached looked to be comprised of mostly middle-aged people. Typically I would get out to help them into the vehicle, but due to the street, it wouldn't have been safe to do so.

The rear passenger door opened, and a bright smile greeted me alongside a rich southern accent. There are three accents that I enjoy hearing repeatedly: Australian (though not the Siri or Alexa version), British (especially the Siri version), and Southern USA. I knew that I was in for a real treat, but I had no idea how much.

"Good evening, sir," the first woman said. The warm tone instantly put me at ease.

"Good evening," I replied. I glanced at the screen to verify the passenger's name. "Samantha?"

I noticed that my own reply took on a hint of southern accent. This was unintentional and felt awkward, but I could tell my passengers were used to it. A lifetime ago, when I lived in Upstate New York, I had a roommate from Alabama. For two months I spoke with a nearly unintelligible hybrid accent of

Northeastern and Southern. Thankfully for everyone, I recognized my linguistic faux pas this time and corrected it right away.

"Yes sir," she replied.

The group pushed towards the vehicle, and after a quick count I could see six people ready to enter. Samantha started probing the seat to figure out how to access the back row.

"Pull the top lever," I directed. For the record, there are three levers marked on the seat and almost no one pulls the right one on the first try.

As she followed the instruction, the seat slid forward and the whole group offered a collective "ooh," as if they had just witnessed the discovery of fire. Two people climbed into the back (Dave and Jessica), three into the middle (Linda, Melissa, and George), and one into the passenger seat (Samantha). Everyone seemed overly cheerful and a little giggly.

"Is everyone in?" I asked. I used the rear-view mirror to check the status on the passengers. I knew from the closed doors that we had everyone, but I checked anyways. I noticed that everyone was dressed very nice and coordinated. The theme color running through the group was a darker red. I wasn't sure if it was purposeful, but it made them look like a group of friends.

"I would say so," Samantha answered on behalf of the group. With that, I tapped my phone to confirm that the passengers had been picked up. The screen quickly changed to navigation with the map and arrow.

"Alright, here we go," I said as I shifted into gear, and clicked off the hazards. I watch the busy road for an opening. It was surprising to have an opening to get on the road as quickly as it came.

"Sir, that is a mighty fine hat you have," Dave said.

"Thank you," I replied, tipping my charcoal gray fedora. It was a common complement to my outfit that helped me stand out not only while driving, but also during the variety of projects I volunteered for. My repeating passengers, all four of them, all told me that they recognized the hat before they recognized my face.

"I have one just like it," Dave said. He enthusiastically made a gesture as if he was putting on a hat.

"Do you really?" Jessica asked. The surprise in her voice cautioned me to doubt his claim.

"No, but now I really want one," he said with a chuckle. Jessica laughed boisterously.

"How much did you two have to drink?" Samantha asked. I could tell that Samantha wasn't just the person who paid for the ride, she was also the ringleader.

"A glass of wine," Jessica said. She quickly giggled a little just after the statement.

"More or less," Dave added.

"Yeah, it was definably more," Samantha said. The group's chemistry didn't just seem playful; I was beginning to suspect that they were pretty much best friends. Which led me to wonder what brought this group of well-dressed southern-speaking people to Utah.

"Where are you from?" I asked.

"Tallahassee," Samantha answered. "Have you ever been there?"

"I haven't, but I would like to at some point," I replied. It wasn't just rhetoric for conversation; as someone interested in history, the East Coast, and especially the Southern East Coast, is on my list of places to visit.

"Well, tell you what, Tallahassee is the best place in the state to visit," Samantha said. The pride in her voice was beaming.

"Unless you're a Disney fan," Linda said as an afterthought.

"Well, yeah, but Orlando is way overpriced. Too busy, too commercial. Tallahassee is the place to be," Samantha offered with a wink. Ironically, I had been to Orlando; my son was a Make–A–Wish kid and Disney World was his wish. (It was amazing, by the way.)

"That's right," Dave said.

"You should visit; you can stay at my place," Samantha said. I had no doubt that her offer was genuine; part of me wished I could take her up on it.

"My wife and I, along with my five kids?" I asked. Knowing that it was going to elicit a big response, I followed the comment with a big grin.

"Oh, my lord, five kids?!" Samantha said. "Is that why you have such a big vehicle?"

With three of my kids being teenagers, I had heard just about every kind of response you could think of when it came to people discovering how many kids I have. The best one being the response from voice actress Tara Strong, who said, "Five kids?! That's crazy!" She said it in the voice of Raven from Teen Titans. It was pretty awesome.

"Exactly," I replied.

"So, this must be exactly what it is like when you are driving your kids around?" Dave asked. Again, he laughed.

"Similar," I said, "but not quite."

"Dad, Jessica is touching me," Dave whined.

"Are we there yet?" Linda asked, also whining.

"I have to use the bathroom," Melissa added.

"Oh boy," I said. The whole vehicle erupted into laughter.

"Hey, what is your favorite song?" Samantha asked. To be honest, this was the first and only time in my Rideshare ride history that I had been asked that question.

"I have many," I replied. This was a real reply; I love a broad range of music. Though if you have read the stories before this one, you know that I especially love Depeche Mode's "Enjoy the Silence."

144 § Jared Quan

"Of course, I can just start singing my favorite," Samantha said. This wouldn't be the first time a passenger broke out into song, but none had announced it beforehand.

"Sure. I am good with whatever song you like," I replied.

I assumed that it would be a halfhearted attempt to sing, the way most of us do, but I was wrong. Samantha started. The rest of the people joined in. Before I knew it, they were in the middle of the Hugh Jackman verse of "A Million Dreams," and sounded amazing. The timing and harmony were perfect. It seemed professional. Right on cue, the group stopped and then erupted into laughter and clapping.

"Wow, that was unbelievable," I said. At this point I had chills from the performance. It was unbelievable, and nothing could have prepared me for that.

"Pretty good. She is the best," Dave said.

"Oh?" I asked. I couldn't help my curiosity as to what this group had achieved with those voices.

"We are all professional singers. We're in town visiting the university," Samantha said.

"No kidding, that is incredible," I said. "I haven't met many professional singers. Your group is stunning."

"No kidding," Samantha said.

"If he thinks that is stunning, let's sing him your favorite, Samantha!" George said.

"Yeah!" The others chimed in.

Then the group started singing again, this time a surprising selection from Britney Spears' 1999 hit song, "Baby one more time."

"That was absolutely brilliant," I said. They sounded fantastic despite the acoustics of the Dodge Journey and the background noise of traffic and driving.

"I love you guys. I wish I could go with you to Tuscany next month," Melissa said, her voice sad. I even thought I heard a sniffle.

"Holy cow, Melissa talks," Linda said.

"Yes; that is because she's drunk," Dave said.

"Hey, I talk when I am not drunk," Melissa said. "I just happen to talk a little more when I am tipsy."

Again, laughter filled the vehicle. I slowed and turned into the hotel parking lot.

"Aw!" Everyone said in unison. I felt the same way. I would have spent the whole night hanging out with them, listening to them sing, if I could.

"We were just starting to have fun," Samantha said.

"I know, and I would love to keep the party going, but I already have another pickup waiting," I said. I could see on the app that I had been assigned another ride even before this one had been dropped off. This was typical on a busy Friday night.

"You are a gentleman and would fit in well in Tallahassee; do come visit us," Samantha said.

I got out to help everyone exit the vehicle and reset the seats. The group slowly started to make their way towards the entrance of the hotel.

"For the record, that hat is truly amazing. You look incredible," Dave said. "I for sure am going to get me one of those."

"Thank you," I said. "You would look awesome."

I waited a minute just to make sure they didn't forget anything. As I looked around, I could hear them singing at the top of their lungs as they entered the hotel. I knew I would never forget the Tallahassee Six.

Two Weddings and an Ex-Husband's Address

It was a late evening on a Saturday. It had been an above average day of driving, and I was looking to knock off early, with just a couple of quick rides more. I got the call to head from downtown Salt Lake City to Bountiful. The drive was longer than I'd expected: the pickup location was high on the mountain overlooking North Salt Lake.

I approached a giant mansion of a house. Cars packed the road. There was a massive sign on the front of the house: a wedding. As I pulled up, what appeared to be a woman was laying facedown on the front lawn. Her shoes were in the grass nearby.

As usual, I confirmed with the app that I had arrived, and it sent a notification to the passenger. The destination address was in Layton, which was a decent fare.

Nobody emerged or approached my car. The timer on the app ran down, and I opted to call them. It rang a while before going to voicemail. Coincidentally, the woman on the lawn had a phone: it lit up at the same time I tried to call my passenger. I tried again. This time, she slowly lifted her head and answered the phone.

"Hello? Who is this?" The woman asked.

"Jessie, this is Jared. I am your ride," I said. Oftentimes when I collected passengers from a wedding they came in groups, so I wondered if it would be just the one passenger.

"Oh, yeah, where are you?" she asked. The tone in her voice seemed really tired and slightly slurred.

"I am at the edge of the driveway. I will flash my brights so you can see me." My brights were probably going to be overkill since she was only about fifteen yards away, but you can never be too safe. I flickered the lights.

"Oh, I see you," she said.

I noticed that she had not made an attempt to get up from the ground yet. "Awesome, do you need assistance?"

"Um, no, I need to get my friends from inside," she replied.

"Okay, I will be waiting." Since I had talked with her, I went ahead and selected the start ride option in the app.

I watched as she slowly peeled herself up off the lawn and staggered her way into the house. After a few minutes she emerged with two other people. They seemed to be holding each other up. Jessie looked right at me, and then started guiding the group in a different direction. Confused, I call her phone again.

"Hello? Who is this?" she asked

"Yes, this is Jared your driver again," I said.

"Where are you? Did you move?"

The question caught me off guard. I had driven my share of inebriated passengers, but I had not run into this kind of scenario before where they couldn't find me. As a side note, even with all of the vehicles parked around, mine was the only one that had its headlights on. Not to mention the glowing rideshare device that identified me.

"No, I am still at the driveway. I will flash my brights again," I said.

I flickered the switch just as I had done previously.

"Oh, we see you," she said with excitement.

The trio managed to make their way over to me. I got out to help them into the vehicle. That is when I noticed that all three were soaking wet. I kept some small hand towels in the Journey while driving, just in case of possible situations like this.

"Hi, I am Jared," I said.

"This is Tonya and Heather," Jessie introduced.

"Good to meet you. I have some hand towels; would you like to use one?" I asked.

"Yes please," Jessie said.

By the time I walked to the back of the Journey and retuned with the towel, Tonya, Heather, and Jessie had all removed their dresses. They were now only wearing bras and underwear. I handed towels to the three shivering mostly-naked women.

"I am sorry, can you put your clothes back on?" I asked. It was a rule that I had put into place after experiencing several situations where people wanted to ride naked or mostly naked. I couldn't for the life of me figure out why people thought that would be okay.

"Oh, we are fine. These are swimsuits," Tonya said as she tugged on her bra, revealing more than I wanted to see.

I am no fashion expert, but I was very certain that they were not swimsuits. I also wasn't about to argue with passengers, and they had kind of covered up with the towels.

"Okay?" I said. "Do you want me to go grab your shoes from the grass?"

"No, I will get them tomorrow, when I pick up my car," Jessie said. This was a very common statement from people being picked up from bars or parties. I got back in and put the vehicle in gear.

"Oh, you look so fancy," Heather said. The three women giggled at the comment.

"Thank you," I said.

Almost instantly, Tonya was asleep. As we began to drive, Heather and Jessie started rambling incoherently.

"Thank you for picking us up," Jessie said. She leaned forward enough for me to tell she was not wearing a seatbelt.

"I am glad I am able to," I said. "Don't forget to put on your seatbelt."

The last thing I needed was to end up in a collision while people didn't wear their seatbelts.

"You are such a nice guy." Heather's voice was soft and flirty at this point. She was now also leaning forward, as if to compete with Jessie.

"Thank you for saying so," I said. It wasn't the first time someone had made an advance on me while driving, and I doubted it would be the last. It wasn't hard for me to shrug it off.

"I am in sales, and it really pays to have great customer service. I really appreciate it," Heather said. I shifted in my seat a little because her breath had brushed against my neck. That was a little too close.

"No problem," I offered. "Is there any chance you can both sit back? I just want you to be safe."

"Hey, can I smoke in here?" Jessie asked.

"I would rather you not smoke." I was grateful that she had asked. I had several people who just decided to smoke or vape without permission.

"Oh, okay," Jessie said. Then, despite the denial of her request, she attempted to light a cigarette. After a few tries, she frowned at her lighter. I was thrilled that the lighter didn't work.

"Sheesh, it looks like I am out," Jessie said. She shoved the cigarette and lighter into her little clutch.

"That sucks," Heather said. "I bet Jared here can help."

"Jared, can we stop to get some beer and a lighter," Jessie said. "We will make sure it is worth your while."

This was one of the most typical requests as a driver. The fees are calculated partly on time and distance from objective, so stopping typically yielded an extra seventy-five cents, plus an extra dollar or two in tips.

"We can make a really quick stop," I said, "but you are going to want to put something on besides your swimsuit."

"Thanks, you are the best," Jessie said. She slipped her dress back on.

"You know what, I want to make sure you are taken care of," Heather said. She looked through her small clutch and pulled out a twenty-dollar bill. "Here you go."

"Thank you, I really appreciate it," I said. As I did with cash tips, I quickly slid it into the left-hand interior pocket of my suit coat. Fun fact: a lot of the loose change in my car was from passengers who tipped in cash. I liked to use it buy snacks or drinks while I was out.

I pulled over to a smaller gas station. It didn't look busy, but the two parking spots were all taken, so I parked next to a pump.

"I will be right back," Jessie said. I noted that she was entering the gas station barefoot and her dress wasn't done up all the way in the back.

She seemed to have more composure than when I picked her up. I watched carefully as she entered the gas station. I turned off the vehicle to save gas.

"Are we there?" Tonya said. Her eyes barely opened.

"No, just at a gas station," Heather said.

"Oh good, I think I need a thing," Tonya said. Just as she finished saying that, she went back to sleep.

"Thank you for taking good care of us," Heather said. "I want to make sure you are taken care of."

She then began to look in her small clutch again and pulled out another twenty-dollar bill.

"Oh no, you already gave me a twenty," I said.

"No, this is on top of that," Heather said.

"I appreciate it, but I am good," I said.

"You really are the nicest guy. I need to date more guys like you," she said. "Thank you."

Unsure on how to best respond to that, I offered, "Anytime."

"This was our second wedding in two weekends, and you are way better than our driver last time. We almost didn't use rideshare and waited for a friend to take us," Heather said.

"I am glad you gave us another chance," I said.

I looked over at the gas station to see Jessie standing at the counter with the beer. Also, there were six different guys talking to her. I didn't like the situation at all. On top of that, there were only two vehicles in the small gas station, and I hadn't seen anyone inside before Jessie went in. I mean, where did all those guys come from?

"I will be right back; stay here," I said.

"Where are you going?" Heather asked.

"To get Jessie."

I promptly walked into the gas station to hear laughter and a guy asking for her phone number.

"Sorry guys, she has to come with me," I said. Instantly the six guys offered me a dirty glare. Even the cashier seemed to join in. I wasn't normally a brave person, but I was certain the situation needed to end.

"Oh, guys, this is my driver, Jared," Jessie said. She blew me a kiss.

"Hey, Jared, let her be," one of the guys said. The guy took a step closer to me.

"We're just talking here," another said. He threw his hands into the air.

"Did she already pay?" I asked. I was super nervous that I was going to get the crap kicked out of me. That would have been so much harder to explain to my wife.

"Yes," the cashier said.

"Okay, then, have a good evening gentlemen." I offered Jessie my hand. She took it and I grabbed the beer and bag she had on the counter.

"Bye!" Jessie said in a cute voice.

I carefully guided her out of the gas station. As we approached the Journey, something looked off. I quickly discovered that Heather was standing in her "swimsuit" filling up my gas intake at the pump.

"Heather?" I asked. "What are you doing?"

"Huh?" she asked.

"What are you doing?" I asked again. I opened the door for Jessie and glanced back at the gas station to see if any of the guys were following.

"I am filling it up with gas, it was almost empty," Heather said with a frowny face.

"There is plenty of gas; go ahead and stop." I shook my head.

"I want to make sure you are taken care of," she said.

I pulled out the twenty from my she had given me earlier. "Okay, let's do this: here is your twenty dollars for the gas."

"Oh no, you keep that." She pushed it back at me.

"Okay. Let me take it from here, please," I said.

She stepped away from the pump and got back into the vehicle. I promptly stopped the fueling. Sure enough, she had chosen the premium gas. Also, I felt bad because the gas station was on the high side of gas prices at the moment. A couple of guys were now standing outside the gas station looking at me. I promptly climbed back into the vehicle.

"Those guys were nice," Jessie said.

"I am sure they were." I started the vehicle and fastened my seatbelt. Deep down inside I had hoped that the guys were not going to try and follow.

"Oh, did you make new friends?" Heather asked.

"You know, I did, but I didn't get a chance to give them my number," Jessie said.

"Good," I mumbled out loud.

After a few minutes we drove into a townhouse complex, and just a few doors down was the destination listed on the app.

"It looks like we are here," I said.

"Oh no." Heather was in a panic. I feared that she had forgotten something at the gas station.

"This is my ex-husband's place; I must have entered it on accident," Jessie said.

Frantically, she shuffled through her phone to figure out how to correct the mistake. I pulled out of the driveway and down the street so that the ex wouldn't see her.

"We can call another ride," she said, working her phone.

"That would be more expensive. We can wait until you have the right address," I offered. The fee for ridesharing is base charge plus distance plus time; at this point they would be paying the base charge again.

A moment later, a ding from the app indicated that the destination had been updated.

"Oh good, I finally got it," Jessie said.

"Alright, we are on our way," I said.

The new drop off point was located only a few blocks away. As I pulled up to the correct address, the two women woke up Tonya. I got out and helped them exit the vehicle.

"I am going to wait here until you are all three safe inside," I said.

"You are the sweetest," Jessie said.

The three women got out of the Journey. I got back into the driver seat and watched as Heather punched in a code on the door several times. Briefly, I wondered if this was the right house, but then they opened the door.

I was about to put the Journey into gear when Jessie walked out of the house and back over to my window. She knocked on it. I rolled it down.

"Hey, I have a secret to tell you," she said.

"Oh?" I asked.

"I am going to whisper it into your ear," she said.

I hesitated for a moment. I truly wasn't sure why she would want to tell me a secret, or if it would be a good idea to play along. After a moment, I turned my ear to her and leaned out the window. I could feel her breath against the side of my face. Then, unexpectedly, she kissed me on the cheek. I pulled back, genuinely shocked. A big smile crossed her face.

"Here, this is for you," Jessie said. She raised her hand to brandish another twenty-dollar bill.

"That's okay; Heather already tipped me," I said.

"Well, this is from me. I wish I could give you more, and I really hope I get to see you again," she said.

"It has been great," I said.

Jessie joined her friends at the door. I watched as they entered the house and the door closed. I pulled away and drove away from the house. I remembered that they were soaking wet. So, I pulled over and checked the seats and towels. Sure enough, there was no way I could take any more passengers for the rest of the night.

I turned off the app and headed for home. Shortly after hitting the freeway, I got the notification of a five-star review and a fifty-dollar tip.

During my time driving, I had my share of people from weddings. Typically, they were a little tipsy, but not over-the-top drunk. Most of those experiences are crazy; this one was, by far, the most unforgettable.

Unscheduled Stop Susie

I once picked up a young woman named Susie,
who wasn't the first passenger I had picked up who was a little
    woozy.
"I have a stop to make on the way," she said,
without hesitation I simply nodded my head.

After all tips often followed the accommodating,
and we get paid for the waiting.
"Oh this smoke shop on the right."
I pulled into the parking lot without a fight.

She raced into the building with questionable balance,
I waited out of rideshare-driver valiance.
Susie quickly reentered the Dodge Journey;
I promptly continued with the directions I see.

"Just one more stop, pretty please."
Once I nodded my head to appease.
"Just a quick stop at the gas station ahead."
I could easily see the requests' common thread.

I pulled up in front of the convenience store,
she entered then exited the front door.
"Can we just make one extra stop,
and I will make sure to take care of you on the tip."
What else could I say but yes as rideshare's ambassadorship.

"Just the McDonalds drive through, I am famished."
I pulled into the drive through in fear the tip might vanish.
"Two McDoubles," ordered Susie;
it didn't seem like she was being choosy.

Finally I dropped her off at her home,
and I drove away all alone.
I watched intently for the tip on the app,
and quickly learned that I was the sap.

No tip ever populated from the fare;
at least I got Susie home with great care.
I don't mind all the extra stops,
McDonalds, convenience store, and smoke shop.

It is my job to get you where you need to go safe and sound,
and tip or no I promise I will be around.

Nauseous Nathan

I picked up Nathan on the far-west reach of West Jordan city,
he promptly said to head to the airport and quickly.
As I drove he seemed especially withdrawn,
my attempt at conversation was answered with a yawn.

Contempt to complete the ride in silence,
the only sound in the car the GPS guidance.
He started to look in his backpack,
I suspected he was looking for a snack.

Then in the most dramatic fashion,
Nathan shouted to pull over, gesturing with great passion.
Promptly I pulled to the side of the road,
the cars on the freeway around us slowed.

He leapt from the car to the median,
in that moment I hoped he wasn't a tragedian.
Nathan proceeded to empty his stomach contents;
I couldn't help but reflect on the turn of events.

After a minute he climbed back into the car,
and signaled to keep going since the destination wasn't far.
Nathan assured me he was just fine,
I couldn't help but hope things would work out for him on the
    airline.

Reaching the end destination,
I worried for all of those going on vacation.
I watched as he walked towards the airport doors,
managing to throw up on the inside floors.

If you are traveling tonight,
I wish for you to have a good (and illness free) flight.

Eavesdropping and Observations

As a rideshare driver, it is impossible not to hear what people are saying. People forget that sound travels forward; I can hear them better than they can hear me from the driver's seat.

I have learned secrets about people cheating on other people. I have heard people badmouth other people, co-workers, and companies. It's almost as if people really don't care because they don't know me, and I don't know them. Sometimes I think they say stuff because they want people outside their circle of friends to know.

People have confessed stuff to me almost like I was a priest at confession. That isn't eavesdropping, but it is fascinating to observe the way they are acting, how they are saying things, and where they are being dropped off.

An article in the Harvard Magazine was curious as to why people tell strangers their secrets.[ii] The data they produced showed that 45% of confidants were people that the study group did not consider personally important. Which means: not family or friends. For one thing, people are worried about how the information might affect their relationships; but the stress of carrying it on their own is too much.

There was a couple I collected from a very nice restaurant. The two seemed enamored with each other. Their very physical contact and close proximity while even in the vehicle suggested a very strong relationship. Then the woman started talking about how the man's wife didn't respect him. Their drop point was a very nice hotel. It was bizarre to me that she said it. It wasn't a conversation I expected, and I was always puzzled as to why she chose that moment to say that. Surely from their interactions, they already had a good understanding of why they were making the choices they were at that time. It was also crazy because I had no stake in their story, nor did I even know a fraction about them.

I found I was quick to judge. But less the people, and more the situation. I imagined what that would look like if that were me or my wife cheating on the other. I had to remind myself that it wasn't me so I could wash my hands of the entire thing.

There was an instance where I picked up a passenger that I knew from one of my many other jobs. They were super embarrassed because they were being dropped off at a place that some people look down on. In this instance, I did have a little bit of a stake in the situation. I had the power to reveal the secret to others or not. I assured them that I wouldn't let other people we work with know because it isn't any of my business or theirs.

It reinforced the fact that people are multifaceted, and often we only see one aspect and judge them on that.

On one occasion, I was terribly irritated with what I had overheard and eventually discovered. I picked up two passengers from a community college. They were carrying two bags of baking ingredients. While I was driving, the two were talking to each other and laughing. I could feel and hear something hit the floor of the back seat.

One of the girls said, "I can't believe that happened."

The other responded, "Should we try to clean it up?"

The first girl replied, "No, it's not our problem."

I knew exactly what had happened and gave them a chance to fess up. I asked, "Is everything okay?"

"Yeah," they replied.

I dropped the two girls off at their destination.

I immediately drove to the closest car wash with vacuums. Sure, enough all over the floor was half a bag of spilled flour. This was a moment that I was really happy that drivers have the ability to rate passengers. I rated them one star; I would have given three, if they had confessed to the spill. The benefit of rating someone a one star is that you can never be paired with that passenger again. I only handed out maybe five of those during my career.

There was another occasion when I picked up four people dressed in full LARPing gear. Though I had tons of questions, one surpassed all others. I had picked them up in the middle of nowhere. There were no other people or vehicles in sight. The best part was that I ended up dropping them off in the middle of nowhere five miles south from where I had picked them up. Unfortunately, they were so deep in conversation, I never got the chance to ask them anything. I tried to extract information from what they were talking about, but I didn't discover anything.

One of the times that I genuinely thought I was going to be murdered, I drove out to a little town away from everything late at night. The map had me driving on dirt roads until it stopped me at the bottom of a hill. I could see that there were houses at the top of the hill, but I didn't see any lights on. I thought that maybe someone called me out on a prank, or to lure me in the middle of night to the outskirts of a tiny town to kill me.

After waiting a few minutes with no sign of my person, I called the passenger. Rideshare software uses 3rd party phone numbers as intermediaries, so no one has anyone's actual phone number. A voice answered and said, "We will be right there" and hung up. It did nothing to assuage my fears. I then spotted a light traveling slowly down the hill. It was in such a way that I couldn't see who or how many.

The thing that really got me was before the light made it to the bottom of the hill, someone knocked on the passenger window. I about had a heart attack. As it turned out, it was six college girls all dressed up to go to the clubs. They were staying at their parents' cabin. Thankfully, they were not murderers.

Sometimes I would hear something or see something that demanded my involvement. Typically, these situations were less than great.

Sometimes I overheard random information that I found super interesting.

While driving a group of businesspeople, I discovered that Rio Tinto recovers large amounts of rare precious metals from the massive copper mine, but they do not sell them directly to manufactures. They sell them instead to smelting companies.

I overheard a discussion between two brilliant government AI engineers. It quickly turned to a debate about where development is at in the AI world. Funny thing was, the lead engineer paused to make sure I wasn't taking their conversation out of context. He said that AI isn't as progressed as people think. It can do some very specific tasks and specialized things, but nothing near what we typically think of when we hear the term AI.

On the flip side, a group of geneticists visiting Salt Lake for a conference were talking through how Ansestry.com and 23&Me both use the same AI software to tease out the genetic details from their tests. They quickly started talking about how the genetic testing of cancerous tumors could narrow down treatment plans to very specific medicines instead of the full spectrum of meds.

One of the things I loved overhearing was when a group visiting Salt Lake for the first time for a conference, or other type of event, remarked on what they thought of Utah. Every time people would say how amazing and beautiful it is. The always said they would love to come back. I often recommended the view from Ensign peak, which is amazing.

The Russian Mafia

On one of the stormiest days in Salt Lake I had ever seen, the rain poured in hard sheets. It was hard to see the road even with the wipers on full speed. Part of the fault laid in the nonreflective paint the State of Utah uses on their roads. The other part was just the sheer amount of water on the pavement.

I got the notice for a pickup at a nearby bus stop. When I arrived, the rain was relentless. I couldn't see anyone waiting; the bus stop seat was empty.

Then, as though they'd materialized from nothing, three women emerged from the rain at a full sprint. I unlocked the car, but before I could get out to open the doors they'd climbed in. All three were shivering, soaking wet, and absolutely not dressed for the weather.

They wore fitted shirts and miniskirts; the clothes clung as if the fabric was trying to warm itself from the women, instead of the other way around. Beneath all that rainwater, though, the clothes were high end. Noting that, plus their piles of bags, I guessed that they'd been shopping downtown and caught off guard. I recognized some of the stores their bags came from. It made me wonder, if they had that sort of money to spend, how they'd ended up here.

"Oh my gosh, are you okay?" I asked. This was, unfortunately, before I started carrying hand towels in the vehicle; I had nothing to offer them.

"C-c-c-c-cold," the middle one managed to say. She had a thick accent.

"Let me get the heat going for you." I turned up the heat and blasted the air. One of the benefits of the Dodge Journey was that its air conditioning and heater were quick to kick in.

"Th-th-thank you," one of the three whispered from the back seat, shivering hard enough that it came through in her voice. All of them were hugging themselves against the cold, rubbing their arms to scrub them warm.

I checked the app. Thankfully, their destination was nearby. "It looks like we are headed up the hill," I said.

"N-n-n-no-o English," the middle woman said. "Only Russian, pozhaluista."[1]

I nodded. "Okay then, let's get you to your destination."

"Spaséeba."[2]

What I was actually thinking was: holy crap, there's some super wealthy Russian mob boss at the top of the hill and if I look at these amazingly good-looking women dressed in their very expensive clothing the wrong way, this could be the last ride I

---

[1] Translation: Please
[2] Translation: Thanks

give. I looked around several times to make sure I wasn't being recorded for reality TV.

The rain continued to pound the city, heavy enough that driving through it was almost like being in a carwash. I started the slow switchback up the hill. I was taking it slow because of the weather, but also due to construction, a plague that infects nearly every road in Utah.

I occasionally glanced into the back seat to make sure everything was okay, and was relieved to see that they were no longer shivering. About halfway up the hill, I heard something like water pouring onto the floor. I looked back to see the middle woman with her shirt off: she was wringing it dry. Rainwater dripped onto the floor of the Dodge Journey. There was more of the woman visible than I was comfortable seeing. I was startled. I was even more surprised that she kept going after our eyes met, zero embarrassment on her end.

"Please don't do that," I stammered. I am certain there was a little panic and embarrassment in my own voice. There were stories out in the rideshare community of things like this, but I never expected it to happen to me.

"No?" she asked. She held her shirt up as if to verify what I was requesting.

I shook my head to emphasize the reply, "Please no."

"Okay," she said. She offered an innocent look and stopped.

Happy that the situation was over, I glanced down to see that we had eight more minutes before our estimated arrival at the destination. After a couple of minutes, I could barely make out some whispering from the back. I glanced in the mirror to see the women talking to each other. Then it sounded like the heater was no longer blowing in the back of the vehicle. I glanced back this time to see that the other two women had removed their shirts and were pressing them up against the air vents attempting to dry them.

I sighed. Though they were not wringing out their shirts, I had hoped they would have understood that I wanted them to keep their shirts on.

"Please don't do that," I said, catching myself blushing.

"No?" the middle woman asked. She held up her shirt as if the action was natural.

I let out a deep sigh and again shook my head the emphasize the response, "Please no."

"Okay," she said again.

I carefully glanced into the rear-view mirror, relieved to see that they were putting their shirts back on. They resumed whispering to each other in Russian, interspersed with giggling.

As we reached the top of the hill, the rain finally slowed to a trickle. My imagination reminded me that, in the movies, this was the scene where mob bosses waited with their henchmen outside their giant houses. I tried to push it from my mind. My overactive imagination would have none of it, and kept bringing it back.

We passed house after house. Each building was bigger than the last, their sizes growing in big jumps. Eventually we came to a massive newbuild just as the rain stopped and the app dinged. I let out a deep sigh of relief as my imagination retreated.

I jumped out and opened the door for the three. They climbed out one at a time, each saying "Bol'shoy spasibo."[3]

The last one turned and blew me a kiss before heading to the door.

All I could think was, "I saw nothing, I know nothing."

I waited just a moment to make sure the women made it into the house safely. Then I checked the seats and confirmed that they were absolutely soaked. There was no chance I would be able to pick up any more passengers. So I got back in, logged out of the app, and backed the Journey out of the driveway. It was at this moment that I found a scenic viewpoint of the valley, and stopped to grab a couple of pictures. One of them became my all-time favorite of all the photos I have taken while driving rideshare.

---

[3] Translation: Thank you very much.

Days of Our Lives

While out driving late one evening, I dropped off a ride in Magna, and quickly got a request to pick up a ride out at Saltair. It was a little exciting because the app let me know that the ride was going to be longer than 45 minutes. That was good fare.

I knew there was a concert happening out there, but it was far too early for it to be over. That made traffic light. I approached the building with little trouble and quickly spotted the requested ride.

I slowed to a stop and got out and opened the door for the two people.

"Aaron?" I asked.

"Yup," Aaron said.

A very physically fit man and woman in their mid-twenties got into the Dodge Journey. I caught a hint of alcohol from the two, but I could tell they were not drunk. The air was thick with tension, and my instincts told me to not ask my usual questions. Each sat on different sides of the vehicle looking out their respective windows.

As I pulled away headed for Bluffdale, the couple began arguing.

"Give me back my phone please," Stephanie said. It was clear from her tone of voice that this wasn't the first time she'd made the request, and frustration had set in.

"No," Aaron fired back. He sounded just as angry as she did.

"I don't understand what the big deal is; just give me the phone back," she pleaded. I didn't need to look to know that there were tears in her eyes.

"Sure, just admit that I caught you." He was direct and challenging, just below a shout.

"You're blowing this out of proportion; you just caught me texting Jessica." She attempted to reach for the phone.

"I caught you texting Jessica… about sleeping with another guy." This time his voice was a little broken and hurt.

"Jessica was just asking if I could remember a guy we went to high school with," she said with a softer tone.

"I saw the text; she was saying you should take off with another guy." He sniffled a little as he started to cry.

"No, she was asking if I remembered this guy Jeff we went to high school with." Her voice wavered as she was fully crying now too.

"Like I would believe that?" he said just above a whisper.

"You should, because it is the truth. Now just give me the phone, and let's move past this. Please," she said, gently.

There was a long pause, and I could see that he was considering giving the phone back. He looked out the window and then looked at the rose gold device in his hand.

176 § Jared Quan

"I will give you the phone back if you unlock it and we go through it together," he said, pushing the words through his tears with something of his former bite.

"You're being paranoid. Just give me my phone please," she said, just as sharp.

"Not going to happen, unless we look through it together."

"Quit acting like an unreasonable jerk!"

"Like a jerk? Me? It's okay for you to give me a Xanax so I pass out so you can go through my phone, but I am being an unreasonable jerk?" Aaron demanded.

I couldn't believe what I was hearing. If this was true, it was an admission to a crime. For a moment I thought through several scenarios, all of which involved me testifying in court, none of which I wanted any part of.

"You keep saying that because I caught you cheating on me with Heather!" Stephanie said.

It wasn't a clear admission or a denial of the previous accusation. I shook my head, wondering if they realized that I could clearly hear everything they were saying.

"It wasn't cheating because we were broken up," he said, slowly and concisely. It seemed like he was wanting to drive that as the heart of his argument.

"The day after we broke up? Just before Valentine's Day," she challenged. Now there was fire in her voice. I imagined Aaron and Stephanie in a court room trying to sway a jury.

"Is that when you first got with Jeff?" he countered.

"I've never been with him; I just knew him from high school," she said, throwing her hands into the air.

"That's it. Driver, pull off Bangerder and drop me off at Jordan Landing, and take her to

the drop off point," Aaron said.

"What?" Stephanie said.

I was elated at the request; the tension was growing to a very uncomfortable level. And I was concerned that it would devolve into a physical confrontation. Silently, I exited Bangerder and pulled up to the gas station at Jordan Landing. Aaron jumped out, followed quickly by Stephanie. I had the impulse to drive away as the two started to shout at the top of their voices.

Two police officers exiting the Maverik gas station paused to listen. One of the officers pointed at me, then them. This was one of the worst-case scenarios that I had gone through in my mind. I wasn't sure how I could get out of testifying in court. I could hear myself saying…

"Yes, he mentioned the possibility of being drugged by Stephanie, and he was keeping her phone from her." Yup, not going to be fun.

The two officers walked to my car. Stephanie and Aaron continued to fight, chasing each other now around the parking lot. I rolled down my window.

"So, what is the deal with the couple?" the first officer asked.

"I picked them up from a concert out at Saltair. It seems like they might have had a few drinks; they have been fighting since I picked them up," I said. "He has her cell phone and won't give it back to her."

"Are they married?" the second office asked.

"I don't think they are. It seems like they are just dating, from what they said." I really wasn't sure; but from the back and forth about breaking up, the conclusion seemed reasonable.

"You're sure about that," the first officer asked.

"I am pretty sure," I said, making it more of a question than an answer.

"Thank you for the info; we better go break this up," the second officer said. I couldn't tell if he was prompting the first officer or if he was indirectly letting me know that I could leave.

I watched from a distance as the two officers approached the arguing couple. I could hear Aaron shouting at the officers. Though I wasn't able to hear the exact words, I had a good idea of what the core of the exchange was. That was because after a few sharp exchanges, Aaron made an uncoordinated effort to push past them. It seemed like he was trying to get back to my vehicle when he shoved one of the officers.

The officer gracefully put Aaron into handcuffs and placed him into the back of the cop car. Instead of calming down, he became enraged.

"You think this is over!?" Aaron shouted. "You think we are still going to Bangkok after this?! It is over!"

The officer promptly moved him to the back seat of the car. It seemed to escalate Aaron even further. Even though no one could hear him, he was clearly shouting at the top of his lungs and flailing about.

The officers talked with Stephanie for a few minutes. I considered taking off when she proceeded to walk over to the Dodge Journey and opened the door, tears streaming down her face.

"Can you take me home?" she asked.

In all the drama, I had totally spaced ending the ride on the app. I was still being paid to drive her. "Yes, I can get you home safely," I said. I looked out the window at the officers, and they waved me off. I sighed in relief that the situation was coming to an end.

"Thank you," she said through her sobs. She verified the address, and we headed off. The rest of the ride was silent. There were about a dozen times where I nearly said something, but a heartbreaking glance in the rear-view mirror kept quiet. The entire time she looked out the window softly sobbing. We arrived at a massive well-lit home, with two Ford Raptors sitting in the driveway.

"Thank you, again, and I am so sorry for that," she said, just above a whisper. She exited the vehicle and walked into her house. I shook my head as I drove away from the most dramatic ride I had given.

Raging Bull

I was called to a popular downtown bar on a Friday evening. I had given dozens of rides from this familiar spot. As I pulled up, I reported my arrival. There was a small group of five men milling about, and one of them looked up for a moment. The five min waiting time ran out, so I pushed the button to call the passenger. This didn't happen often and most of the time it was understandable, but this time was very annoying. The passenger answered the call and, sure enough, it was the one who had looked up at me when I had arrived.

"Dude, I will be over in just a min," he said, then quickly hung up before I could say anything. I could see him point and laugh. It was at that moment that I realized: the passenger was finishing up his cigarette. After another few minutes, he finally stumbled over to the Journey. I jumped out to open the door for him, but he was already getting into the vehicle.

"Trevor, right?" I asked. The strong smell of cigarette smoke, alcohol, and body odor oozed from him in a thick cloud. It was powerful enough that I gagged a little on smelling it.

"Yup, that's me," he said with a creepy crooked smile.

"Cool, it looks like we are not too far away from your destination," I said, as I pulled away from the bar. The next destination was, in fact, another bar. This wasn't unusual; people would get cut off at one bar and head to another, or they would have friends at the second or third location waiting for them.

"Yeah, I am headed to the next bar; that one sucked," Trevor said as he let out a long burp.

The sour smell turned my stomach, and I had to do everything to keep my body from reacting to it. I rolled down the windows a little.

"Oh? Why is that?" I asked, trying to be friendly.

"They kicked me out for fighting with another guy," he said, looking proud. He raised his fists and threw a punch at the air.

"Yikes," I offered. I realized that I had not rolled the windows down enough; the wind seemed to be pushing the stronger smell at me instead of away. I wanted to roll them down more, but I didn't want my passenger to get irritated.

"Yeah, I was totally going to beat the crap out of him if they hadn't jumped in and stopped me." He threw another punch at the air. I glanced at him to see that he had a black eye and a bruised cheek.

"Ah," I replied. I was completely unsure of what to say, actually, this was a first for me.

"You know, I can appreciate a man like you. All independent and hardworking, you know?" He leaned towards me.

The stench hit me hard, and I had to try and capture fresh air by turning my head towards the window. I tried to make it look like I was checking the mirror.

I managed to gasp out, "Yeah."

"You know, people have unrealistic expectations. Like my mother, she expects me to go out and domesticate. Doesn't she know that she is hindering my creativity! You know?!" he said. The bitterness and resentment dripped from every word. His facial expression matched his tone.

"Right," I said. It was about this time that I realized Trevor was heavily drunk, and not just tipsy. Though the incohesive rambling was a hint, the slurring brought it home. Interesting fact: you can reek of alcohol but not be drunk at all. Beer and wine are the least intoxicating drinks, but they have the strongest smell.

"Aw man, you know I could have won that fight at the bar. That guy was a loser, you know?" The question seemed rhetorical. I simply nodded. That was when Trevor balled his fists and started punching the air in front of him: one–two, one–two, one–two, bam–bam–bam.

"Oh, man, I feel good! I feel like I need to fight someone." He started to punch the air with more force and intention behind it, almost as if he was going to hit something full speed.

"Woah, woah, I don't want to fight you," I said. This marked a first in my driving career. I had never felt like I was in any sort of danger, but this guy held himself like a threat. As inebriated as he was, anything was possible.

"I won't fight you as long as you agree with me," he managed to say while waving his finger at me.

"Yeah, whatever it is, I agree with you," I said, mostly out of desperation. I didn't feel like I was out of the woods yet. I became very eager to reach his destination and ran a yellow light to reduce the time.

He rolled down the window and shouted as loud as he could, "Good, but I really need to fight something!"

Some poor bystanders on the street were startled by the shouting. Then he began to howl out the window like a wolf.

Thankfully, at that point we arrived. I pulled up to the next bar and stopped at the soonest possible moment. He leaped from the Journey in a full rage. He left the passenger door open, so I hit the gas and then braked hard enough for the door to—barely—latch shut. In that moment, I caught a glimpse of him full-on punching the closest street sign and kicked the pole. I knew instantly I needed to get out of there before he redirected any anger at me.

I was certain that he had broken his hand on the first punch, but he was so out of it he kept on going. As I drove away, I could see people running up to him. I turned the corner and let out a huge sigh of relief that I and the Journey were safe. His stench lingered. I rolled all the windows down, and drove a couple of blocks to air out before pulling over and waiting for my next call.

The Lost Russians

A cute Russian couple from Los Angeles,
visited Salt Lake City with a conference of analysts.
After a mild night of hitting the bars,
the two struck out into the night guided only by stars.

Their destination seemed harmless as they headed for the
    Gateway,
they walked with a little intoxicated sway.
Before they knew it they were down a dark street named Rio
    Grande,
and got into far more than they had ever planned.

Realizing they were lost on a closed off street,
they called up a rideshare hoping for a miracle feat.
The shadows seemed to loom large as time passed;
they hoped and prayed the rideshare would arrive fast.

After an eternity in the dark,
they emerged to enter the ride waiting in park.
Grateful to escape being lost and alone,
so they could finely arrive at their intended drop zone.

Even though their destination lay only a minute away,
they were having an enjoyable field day.
High fives, fist bumps, and hugs abound,
only bright smiles and laughter could be found.

So happy were the cute Russian couple,
they tipped more than the rate but double.
I was happy to rescue the lonely lost pair,
and see that they arrived a happy fare.

I love saving people from all kinds of situations,
escalating frustrations, relations, or starting a weekend vacation.

A Tale of Two Brothers

On a cold dark night two brothers summoned an XL rideshare,
to join some good friends who had just got off their shift.
The driver picked them up while the two sat in silence;
they quickly reached their friend's address, exiting in shyness.

They check the house to discover it's the wrong friend's house,
quickly they called up another XL, egos doused.
The same driver arrived to take them to the next destination set,
thinking for sure the second shot would find their friends yet.

Arriving at the next friends place,
to find no one there so they left in haste.
Calling another XL, third time with the same driver,
they drove with great conversation, this time tipping a fiver.

Super frustrated to not find their friends, they XL again this time
        back to home,
deciding that it was better than to continually roam.
Now nearly best friends with the rideshare driver,
who gave them four back-to-back rides again they drop a fiver.

As the driver of the two brothers,
I must give them a huge thank you for the extra funds
and promise to pass it onto others.

Doppelgänger Daphne

Driving late on a cold Christmas weekend night,
the city sparkling with colorful lights so bright.
I got the summons to pick up a ride,
I rushed to arrive and keep the passenger satisfied.

I offered a warm welcome to the blonde-haired woman,
she reciprocated as a young vibrant human.
There was something that seemed so gosh darn familiar,
I glanced real hard in the rear-view mirror.

"Have I given you a rideshare ride before?"
"No, I don't think so; I would remember your fedora for sure."
"Sounds good, let's get you to your destination."
Still there was something in my mind causing hesitation.

We headed on our way,
It didn't take long before we were on the freeway.
That is when it hit me clear as day,
"You look exactly like a woman I work with every day!"

"Oh really, perhaps we are related."
"Her name is Malinda Lee," I said, elated.
"Sorry, I've never heard of her."
Embarrassed, the rest of the ride seemed like a blur.

After I dropped off Daphne, the doppelgänger of my coworker,
I promptly drove off as to not be a lurker.
I have had many people who so closely resemble people I know,
But none near so identical I had to add the trip to my writing
    portfolio.

Odds and Ends

When it comes to rideshare, the breadth of everything that I have seen and experienced is simply boggling. I wanted to share some short clips of various, miscellaneous things that I found super interesting.

I was used to driving at night during the weekdays, and then the whole day on the weekends. There were people chatting in the Facebook rideshare groups that mentioned a weekday morning rush. I hadn't experienced it for myself. Then, during a job change, there was a window of opportunity. The very first day I tried it, I was extremely surprised. I had daisy chained five back-to-back rides. They were short distance, so low use of gas and higher profit.

On the second day I decided to do a morning drive, I got out at 8:30AM. I instantly got a ride, but it dried up right after that one. I tried to drive to a more populated area to find rides, but everyone was at work. I ended up wasting a bunch of gas. After driving at various times in the morning, I discovered that the rush starts at 6AM and ends at 9AM.

The first time I decided to queue up at the Salt Lake Airport to get rides, I had an eye-opening experience. I discovered that drivers had to wait in areas close to the airport but not on airport property. Many grew fond of a gas station that sat on the edge of the airport. For me, I parked on the side of the road on the Bangerder Highway facing the airport just inside the zone.

During one passenger pickup at the airport, the back end of the Dodge Journey barely hung over the edge of the pedestrian crosswalk. Immediately one of the airport police officers approached me. They explained that they were giving me a warning, and the next time I picked up someone and had any part of the vehicle over the crosswalk I would get ticketed. This was the scenario I was worried about when I picked up the passenger from Napal. In quick discussion with another driver, I found out they had been fined $6,000. After that I was extremely cautious in the airport rideshare pickup zone.

It was really fun to drive during University of Utah football games and Sundance. One of the rideshare companies was an official partner for both, so we got exclusive waiting areas and pickup spots. It streamlined the transit of mass amounts of people. This was very different from the chaos of picking people up from a Utah Jazz game. Some events, like concerts, or various venues throughout the area would designate a special area for rideshare drivers to drop people off to avoid the traffic. This would often pay off for people who didn't want to pay for parking and walk a mile to the event.

As far as educational information goes, there is nothing better than to drive an expert in a field. You get unfettered access to ask questions. I learned that the University of Utah is home to a fully operational nuclear reactor. Vehicles are on the verge of having sensors so advanced that they will be able to brace a vehicle for an impact, reducing damage and injury. And there was this brief conversation:

Me: "What kind of work do you do?"

Passenger: "I work on radars for self-driving cars."

Me: "Oh, so they know when to stop for other cars?"

Passenger: "No, I am working with a team to develop the radar so it knows what is in a paper bag."

Me: "What? Really?"

Passenger: "Yeah, if a paper bag is in the road, you know to drive over it because it is a paper bag, but a self-driving car doesn't know the difference between a paper bag and a brick."

Me: "Oh…"

Passenger: "So the trick is to get the radar to know exactly how dense the material is inside the bag, so it knows if it needs to stop or drive over it."

Me: "Wow, that is super cool, how could you even start to tell it that?"

Passenger: "Actually, I don't think I am supposed to be talking about it."

The glass that is installed at the ski resorts in Utah is over an inch thick, with a space filled with special gas, and then a special half inch thick grouping of thinner sheets of glass all laminated together. There is an industrial x-ray company that makes a machine made specifically to x-ray an entire shipping container in one shot. Microbiologists translate scientific studies into practical information for doctors to utilize.

I honestly don't think I would have stumbled on any of those pieces of information in any other circumstance.

Some of the most interesting things I learned while driving rideshare were about Utah itself. I discovered that it has a very diverse restaurant selection, if you go looking for it. Like a restaurant that serves food from Somalia, or another that serves food from Peru. And I thought I knew how unique people's names were in Utah, but I had no idea. Of the many rides I gave, a large portion were truly unique names, not just normal names spelled in creative ways. I am someone who doesn't go to bars, so it was fascinating to learn that pre-COVID the bars closed at 1AM, and state liquor stores were open Monday through Saturday 11AM to 10PM.

During my time driving, I was given permission by a few Utah authors to give away foreign print versions of their books to passengers who could read them. The first person to give me that idea was Charlie N. Holmberg, author of *The Paper Magician*. I gave away nearly a dozen of her books, in languages from French to German, and one instance of Czech.

It was always fun to discover amazing people who read in another language. Then, at the end of the ride, I could present them with a book as a gift. They were always surprised and grateful. One girl gave me a hug because she said she had didn't have much money and struggled to find books printed in French. One older gentleman was looking for a gift for his granddaughter, and when I gave him a German copy of the book he gave me a hug. (Remember, this is all pre-COVID.)

As an author myself, sometimes the conversation would come back to the books I had published at the time, *Ezekiel's Gun* and *Changing Wax*, and we would talk about writing as well. Everyone was always fascinated when I talked about my five kids, my son's pending heart transplant, the various jobs I held at the same time, and my volunteer work. In the end, a lot of people went onto Amazon to buy *Changing Wax*. They loved showing me the picture of the purchase. Don't tell *Ezekiel's Gun*, but *Changing Wax* is a much better book.

I really enjoyed driving in Park City. It was not only beautiful, but it was very profitable. Park City has a higher rate of pay for rideshare drivers. During one occasion, a week before Christmas, my first ride of the day was from the airport to Park City. Then I stayed up there all day. I made fifteen rides in the area. Between ride fares and tips, I managed to pull in just under $350. That was my best day in Park City.

I took me about 100 rides before I discovered that I wasn't being as efficient as I could have been. When I started, I thought after each ride I should drive back into downtown Salt Lake. As it turned out, that is a huge waste of gas. I started dropping people off and then driving around the corner and waiting. This is a sound practice most of the time. However, I also set a fifteen-minute limit; then I would drive closer to a main road or freeway.

When it came to personal bests, I hit some fun stats:

The most rides I gave in a day was 32.

The most I made in a day was $775.

The most I made on a single ride was on a snowy day from the airport to Heber, for which I made $165 plus the $10 tip.

The shortest trip I gave a passenger was two houses away, just one hundred feet.

The farthest trip was from the airport to Logan—1 hour 30 min—88 miles.

The least I paid for 17 gallons of gas, my average fill up, was $30.

The longest I waited in line at the airport to get assigned a passenger: 2 hours.

The longest I waited in line to drop someone off at an event: 1 ½ hours.

The longest day of driving was 18 hours (12 hours straight then a mandatory 6-hour break and then 6 more hours of driving).

Number of 1-star reviews: 1 (that I know of).

Number of times pulled over by police: 0.

During my time driving, I took tons of pictures. I loved finding those rare spots for great photos. I only had my phone to use, but it paid off so many times. From views of the valley, to nighttime in the canyons with no other vehicles around. It was fun stopping to see the sights. I stopped once to participate in a ghost tour of the Salt Lake City Cemetery with a group of writers. I stopped at historical buildings and sites. Places that I wouldn't typically go because they were out of the way.

One thing that was consistent with driving rideshare was that you never knew what was going to happen next. You never knew where the next ride would take you.

Kindness

One Saturday evening, I was summoned to pick up an XL ride in downtown Salt Lake. I pulled up to a very nice restaurant. Six people exited the establishment carrying several large bags of leftover food. I climbed out to assist the group, opened the back door, and slid the seat forward.

"Marleen?" I asked.

"Yes sir! That is us," she answered. She had a heavy Texan accent. The entire group was in a good mood: boisterous laughter and big smiles told the entire story of how their dinner had gone.

"Awesome! It looks like you are at the hotel just down the street and around the corner," I said. It really was a short distance, but I wondered if it was because of the bags of leftovers that they elected to take rideshare.

"That's right!" she said.

"Perfect! Let's get you loaded up," I said.

In short order, the vehicle was in drive, and we were headed to the destination. Most of the passengers started to settle into food comas.

"Are you from Utah?" I asked. I suspected that they were from out of state, but asking was a good, reliable way to start a conversation.

"No, we are just visiting in town for a conference. We are from the great state of Texas," Marleen said. The passengers cheered with Texas pride, agreeing.

"What kind of conference?" I asked. It was always interesting to hear about the various conferences that take place in Salt Lake. I had seen everything from a Morticians' conference to a conference for Cytopathology.

"It's a tech conference; we're working on software that can figure out what is inside a bag from a picture," she said.

This sounded oddly like the person working on the radar for self-driving cars. However, determining a bag's contents from a photo was a different ballgame from scanning material density with radar.

"Wow, I didn't think that was possible," I replied. I wondered, if they cracked the code, if they could look at old photographs and know what people had been carrying decades past.

"Well, it isn't possible yet, but we are working on it," she said.

"That sounds amazing!" I said, my author's imagination already running away with new ideas and what-if's.

"Thanks, we think so," Marleen replied.

"We should be to your hotel in just a min," I said.

"Actually, we have a problem; we have way too much leftover food," Marleen said.

When she said this, I thought that she was going to offer the food to me. From the number of bags, it seemed like there would be enough to feed a large family. The problem would be that I was in the middle of my night, and it would be impossible to carry both new passengers and the food.

"Oh?" I asked.

"Do you know any place where we can take this and give it to the homeless?" she asked.

The question caught me off guard, but I knew exactly where the perfect spot was. One of the organizations I'd volunteered with was The Kindness Project in Salt Lake. It was run by amazing volunteers (shoutout to Darren Lamb, who is one of them), who make food and hand it out to the homeless. My kids and I had volunteered to help on a weekend before Christmas.

Out of hundreds of rideshares collected from restaurants, none of the passengers carrying leftovers had ever requested help donating it to the needy. "I know exactly where we can go," I announced, already detouring to the place in mind.

"Is it far?" Marleen asked.

"Nope, not far at all," I said. We were only a block away from the large homeless camp. I knew we would need to be careful. With it being later at night and limited food to hand out, we would need to be on the fringe of the main camp.

"We have a lot of food; will there be enough people to eat it?" she asked.

When we handed out food to with the Kindness Project, we had made hundreds of grilled cheese sandwiches and just as many cups of hot chocolate. This food would be welcomed, but if everyone split it, then most would barely get a morsel.

"Oh, yes. Just a little further." I neared the end of the street, right where the homeless shelter sat. Large groups of people were standing around outside when we pulled up.

"There are so many," she said.

I wasn't going to mention that the majority were not out and about at this time. We rolled down the windows and we called some of the people over.

"We have lots of food; make sure to share with as many as you can," I said.

"For sure," a homeless guy said. He called a few others over.

"This is the good stuff," another homeless guy said, just looking at the containers.

"Yes, please enjoy," Marleen said.

"Thank you, and God bless!" another said.

We waited for a few moments and watched as the group split up the food and began to enjoy it. It was a scene that would, in later months, become intimately familiar as I and my kids returned with The Kindness Project carrying soup, grilled cheese, and more hot chocolate.

After a moment, I could tell that my altruistic passengers were ready to head back to their hotel. Many had tears in their eyes and were smiling and crying at the same time.

"Thank you so much for helping us do that!" she said.

"No, thank you for letting me be a part of that; they really needed that," I said.

"No problem!" Marleen said.

I pulled up to the hotel drop off point and stopped in the unloading zone. I got out and helped everyone out of the vehicle. The small group headed into the hotel, beaming with smiles ear to ear. I have seen some very generous people and events in my days; this one ended up being one of my favorites.

The Death Star Trench Run

I was finishing a full Saturday of driving, planning to run one last ride for the night. Trash cans washed down the avenues, pushed along by fierce rain and brutal wind and a river of runoff from the storm. It was kind of funny how they traveled down the middle of the street in a line. I couldn't imagine what I would do if my own trash can took off like that; who would I even call? Would I go out hunting for it like a lost dog?

The whole day, I had collected passengers struggling to stay upright in the wind. Others were exposed to the rain for five steps and entered the vehicle soaked. I had debated switching off the app and heading home, but I was just two rides away from hitting a bonus that would essentially double my profit for the day. I was hoping for two short rides in this weather.

The call I got was for Sugarhouse.

I pulled up to a fantastic cottage-style home. After reporting my arrival, I got the notification that this passenger was headed to Wanship. This was up the canyon, not far from Park City. I had made a trip up to Park City earlier that morning. The snow was just starting up in the mountains when I was there.

An older man and woman emerged from the house. The wind caused the trees to whip back and forth violently. I got out

202 § Jared Quan

to open the door, but I removed my fedora. I was certain it would be lost if I kept it on. I met the couple at the rear passenger door.

"Diane?" I ask for verification.

"Yes," she replied with a big grin.

"Perfect. It looks like we are headed up the mountain?" I asked. Deep down inside, I was hoping it was wrong, and the trip would be much shorter.

"Correct," she replied.

"Take care of this special lady," the older man said. Diane blushed and let out a little bit of a laugh at the statement. Then she kissed him on the cheek.

"Will do," I said, dipping my head in a nod.

"Thank you, Charles, for a wonderful evening," Diane said. Even with the violent wind, the air was thick with the smell of essential oils. It was familiar; Utah houses two of the largest essential oil companies in the world.

"Be safe out there; this weather looks crazy," Charles said. I am certain he was talking to me as he looked at the nearby tree bending and groaning with the wind.

"We will," Diane promised.

I made sure Diane was in a good place before shutting the door. I ran back around and got soaked from the rain. I was fortunate: it was one of the days where I had elected to wear contacts instead of my glasses. It hated trying to clean water off my glasses.

"Have you driven up the canyon today?" she asked.

"Yes," I replied.

"How bad was it?" she asked. I could hear the concern behind her question.

"It wasn't bad, but that was this morning," I said. Utah did a fairly good job of taking care of the canyon road, since it connected Park City with Salt Lake and the airport. Even if the snow was bad, the roads were probably okay.

"Oh, have you driven the canyon when it's bad before?"

It was a fair question, and a valid concern. Passengers want to be confident that their drivers have the skill to handle bad weather.

"Yes, a couple of times." It was a completely honest answer, and I *had* driven the canyon under bad circumstances. But we were about to find out that I had no idea what bad actually looked like.

"Oh good. There is no need to rush; let's just get there safely," she said, as she started typing on her phone.

"I am with you ma'am," I answered.

I put the vehicle in gear and began to drive out of the neighborhood. At this moment, large snowflakes began to fall, creating a slush on the road. I was relying on my limited experience, the all-wheel drive of the Dodge Journey, and the heavy-duty all-weather tires I recently installed.

Entering the freeway, I noticed that there were very few vehicles on the road, but the snowplows were already at work. One passed me spilling salt on the pavement; the small rocks pinged off the side of my vehicle. Before, they'd only been spraying brine.

I wanted to start a conversation with my passenger, but I realized immediately that driving was going to take one hundred percent of my concentration. In just a few minutes' span, I saw no less than five vehicles that had slid off the road. They were all recent, as I could see people trying to figure out what to do while standing next to their cars.

I made the turn from the I–215 onto the I–80, and I was instantly hit with very heavy snow and strong winds. Immediately off to the side of the road were two big rig trucks that looked like they had smashed a truck between them. The highway patrol was on scene with flairs, but it was barely visible. Nothing felt good about the situation I was heading into. I debated on offering to take my passenger someplace else to wait out the storm; but being so close to the end of the night, I figured I could power through.

I gripped the wheel tightly as I started climbing the canyon. The snow was clearly packed and fresh at the same time. Which was a great combination to create an accident. There was evidence that plows had run through here, with mounds off to the left and right of the road. As we got a little deeper into the canyon, the snow began to shift directions with the various cross winds. The snow was coming down so thick that I could not see anyone else's headlights on the road. I swallowed hard as I made one of the first turns. Deep down inside, I was praying hard to stay on the road. I glanced in the mirror; my passenger was still looking at her phone, which was probably smart. As a passenger, I would be panicking a little at what I was seeing.

We'd reached the halfway point up the canyon when two smaller vehicles raced past us. One of the two shrieked from its oversized custom exhaust. I didn't see either of them until they were within twenty yard.

I was grateful that this section of road had three lanes. I was staying in the middle lane to give myself leeway if anything started to slide. The two vehicles fishtailed a little as they cut between lanes.

My breathing intensified as I rounded another corner and it looked like headlights were coming straight at me. I wasn't entirely wrong. One of the two cars was now facing backwards off the side of the road. I wanted to make sure they were okay, but I was certain that it wasn't safe to stop.

My inner Star Wars fan decided that this was what the Death Star trench run had been like. The struggle to stay on course while other vehicles careened around you, knowing at any second things could go belly up. I imagined Obi-Wan's voice saying, "Use the force."

I tried to relax my shoulders a little, but my grip on the wheel was too intense to let up.

As I neared Jeremy Ranch, the snow managed to increase. In my mirror, about twenty yards behind me, large truck headlights approached at great speed. Then, just as quickly as I saw the headlights, they were gone. I don't know if they slowed down or slid off the road. All I knew was that they were no longer there.

After another few minutes, the snow finally gentled, and the roads seemed in better condition.

I slowed as I approached a wreck still on the road. The highway patrol directed me to the righthand lane away from the accident. As I switched lanes, my heart skipped a beat: I could feel the Journey sliding. Carefully I guided it back on course, trying not to over correct.

I passed the Park City turn off, and finally let myself relax a little. My hands ached from gripping the steering wheel tight for so long. I was thankful that the snow had faded off, and the roads were clear. It didn't take long before I was pulling into a long driveway towards a ranch style house. It looked like a picture right out of a Hallmark Card or a scene from a cheesy romance movie. I slowed to a stop next to the large house.

It looked as though she was oblivious that we had arrived. "Is this good?" I asked.

"Perfect," she replied, giving me a cheery smile.

"Thank you for choosing rideshare," I said with a tired and strained voice. I got out and opened the door for her.

"Thank you for getting us up the mountain; that was pretty intense," she said. I was surprised that she had noticed.

"My pleasure," I replied.

She climbed out of the vehicle, and I watched to make sure she made it into the house. As I turned around, I got the notification that Diane was satisfied, with a five-star review and a twenty-dollar tip.

I needed one more ride to hit my bonus, but I wasn't sure that I could make the death star trench run a second time. I felt physically drained from the drive up the canyon. I reached over to go offline when I was summoned to a resort in Park City. I was tempted to ignore the request and try to head home, but I slid the accept bar instead. After all, I had a perfect record of accepting 100% of the rides up to that point. I let out a deep sigh and headed for the next ride. Thankfully I was able to hit my goal that night, and when I headed home, the storm had mostly passed. I made it home with no problems.

Cheese Stick

Here is another of my routines while out driving for rideshare. I would stop by a Maverick gas station to start the shift. There, I'd purchase two large diet sodas, two waters, and five cheese sticks. Sometimes I snagged a beef jerky or two from the container by the register. The Journey had an insulated compartment for stashing things under the passenger seat, so I used it. One of the diet sodas, the two waters, and couple of the cheese sticks went in for later. I kept them for snack breaks and, on days that scorched, for the homeless people whose paths I crossed.

During various times in my life, I was given opportunities to develop more compassion for those in tough circumstances. I had done service as a boy scout for the homeless in Phoenix; I worked at a food pantry and a soup kitchen in upstate New York. In my youth, my parents had my siblings and I take toys to less fortunate families.

Recently, I was fortunate enough to work with an amazing group of people called the Kindness Project, as I mentioned previously. I had gone with my kids to make grilled cheese sandwiches and soup to hand out to homeless people. It was a humbling experience for me and my children. I started arranging my downtown route to pass by some of the more prominent areas when I got the chance, and then hand out what little I had.

On one particular day, I loaded up at the gas station as usual, and then got a call to pick someone up not too far away. I didn't have time to eat any of the cheese sticks, so I stashed them with the rest. The pickup was at a small strip mall occupied mostly by small businesses. I notified the customer through the app. A woman dressed in a business suit approached. I climbed out to open the door.

"Martina?" I asked.

"Yes," she replied.

"Excellent. I am Jared, and I will be your driver today," I said with a tip of my hat.

"Sounds good," she said. I noticed her tall black high heel shoes.

At this moment, another woman came rushing out of the business we were in front of. They exchanged information in a language I didn't recognize. Afterwards, Martina got into the rear passenger seat. I climbed in and looked at the app for guidance.

"It looks like we are headed about three miles away," I verified.

"Yes." Her curt answer felt irritated.

"Perfect," I said with a friendly smile.

I put the vehicle in gear and pulled out of the strip mall. Martina took a call on her cell phone. She was talking fast in another language, which seemed different from the other one she had been talking in previously. I glanced in the mirror, and she was looking back at me in the silvered glass. It was the very familiar 'mind your own business' look, not that I understood what was being said.

Though just a few miles away, the location required us to jump on the freeway for the fastest route. I got into the left-hand turn lane and stopped at the line for a red light.

On the concrete island was an older gentleman with very chapped lips, holding a sign. The sign read, 'Please help, homeless, no family.' He was wearing tattered clothes and an old army jacket. There was a small, worn, green rucksack on the ground next to him. I knew it was over one hundred degrees out there.

Without hesitation, I put the vehicle in park. I opened the passenger seat and retrieved a water bottle and three cheese sticks. I rolled down my window and waved him over.

"Here you go, man, stay safe out here," I said.

"Thank you." His voice was raspy and sounded just as dehydrated as he looked.

I rolled up my window and after a moment the light turned green. I headed onto the freeway.

"Well, that was inappropriate," Martina said. Her voice was quiet, and I wasn't sure if she was still on her phone. I glanced in the mirror and though she was not talking, her phone was still up to her head. It only took a few minutes for us to arrive at a well-groomed residence. The rear passenger door opened before I could ask if this was a good place. Martina climbed out but held the door open for a moment.

"I don't think that it was appropriate to give that homeless person anything," she said.

"Pardon me?" I asked. I was super confused at the comment. I had done that same thing many times with and without passengers, and no one had ever said anything negative. I could understand people looking down on handing out money, but it was water and cheese sticks.

"I don't support that kind of behavior and I will let your employer know about it." She slammed the door and walked into the house.

I was completely baffled by the exchange. I replayed the scenario in my mind, to make sure I didn't miss anything. I was being safe, the light was red, and I hadn't put the passenger at risk. I shrugged it off and drove away from the house.

It was moments later that I received the one-star review and a formal complaint about my behavior. After a moment I got a call from the rideshare company.

"Mr. Quan?" they asked.

"Yes?" I said cautiously.

"We received a formal complaint about you, and we needed to follow up on it before we can let you continue to drive," the person on the other end said.

"Okay." I was nervous that this could get me suspended from driving rideshare. This was an income my family had come to depend on to keep the bills paid.

"It says here that you stopped at a red light, and inappropriately gave food and water to a homeless person. Is that correct," they asked.

"I did stop at a red light, and gave a bottle of water and three cheese sticks to a homeless person," I said.

"Okay, that is all we needed to know," they said.

"Do I get to keep driving?" I asked.

"Oh yes, you are fine to continue driving. I hope you have a great day," they said.

Needless to say, I did not get a tip from that passenger, and it was one of the few times I really didn't care. The complaint did not keep me from continuing to give out bottled water and cheese sticks when I had the opportunity to.

Eviction

It was a rainy Friday afternoon when I was called to an apartment complex fairly close to my day job. When I arrived, a younger woman wearing a green hoodie and dark blue jeans on her cell phone walked up to the vehicle. She opened the door and got in before I could jump out.

"Steph?" I asked.

She replied with a nod, as she was still having a conversation on her cell phone.

I started towards the destination. Rain pattered the windshield. I glanced in the mirror and could see my passenger was crying while on the phone.

"Listen, is there no way you can work with me on this," she said.

"Okay," she said.

"I will see what I can do," she said.

She put the phone down and looked out the window. Tears streamed down her face. I reached into the middle console and retrieved a couple of tissues.

"Are you okay?" I asked as I handed the tissues back to her.

A brief smile crossed her face as she took the tissues. "I don't know." Her breathing stuttered for a moment as she covered her mouth to stifle a sorrowful sound.

"I am so sorry; is there anything I can do?" I knew better than to ask this question. It was the infamous question that everyone asked, and it really meant nothing at all. Normally, I tried to offer something specific, to help the person better understand, and believe, my commitment and willingness to help. In this case, I didn't know what the issue was; I didn't know what to offer.

"I wish. There isn't anything anyone can do at this point," she said quietly.

She dabbed her tears.

I couldn't help but feel sad even without knowing the situation.

"You see, my brother and I received asylum here in the States six month ago, to leave the brutality and bloodshed in our country. We were sponsored by a good friend of my parents, a well-known politician here. They were going to help us get established, but they died just a week after we arrived."

"Oh my gosh." I didn't mean to comment, but it just escaped my mouth.

"My brother and I both found jobs. The people my brother worked with befriended him, but it was soon after that we realized they were troublemakers. My brother was out with them, and the other guys vandalized some expensive property. They were caught and my brother ended up being arrested. They all said my brother did all of the damage. My brother's English is not so good, and the police said he confessed. He had never done anything like that before in his life; he is what you would call a geek here."

"Yeah."

"They let him be on probation, as long as he stays out of trouble and has a stable place to live." She stifled another sorrowful sound and let out a deep breath. "I had to switch jobs to make more money, because no one would hire him. We tried everywhere."

"Oh no," I whispered.

"My new job doesn't pay my first check until next Friday, but we were already behind on rent. So, they are evicting us," she said.

There wasn't anything I could add. A large lump formed in the back of my throat. I tried to imagine the frustration and emotion of the situation.

"That was my brother's probation officer on the phone; they are coming to arrest my brother because we no longer have a stable place to live. He said they can hold him for four hours before he is in jail for breaking probation. So, I have four hours to find a new place to live."

I caught myself tearing up at the situation and story. I cleared my throat.

"Maybe I can help you find a place," I offered. I actually had no idea where I would start to help her look.

"You are kind, but my friends and I have called anywhere there was any kind of opening. They all need a deposit that I couldn't give them until next Friday," she said as more tears escaped her eyes.

"I am so sorry. What are you going to do?" I asked. I wanted to know to see if there was any other place where I could help out.

"I have to say goodbye to my brother before they take him. I will stay with some friends until I get paid, and find a place then," she said.

It dawned on me that I could do something that was helpful. "I will contact the rideshare company to refund this ride, and let them know I want to gift it to you. It is the least I could do."

"No. You are here doing this because you have to. You are probably driving to provide for a family; having this little amount won't change my circumstances, but for you it adds up," she said.

I was speechless as I pulled up in front of a small house that had been divided into apartments. The landlord was already well underway placing Steph's belongings on the small unkept lawn. At this moment, I was filled with of all sorts of emotions. I was ready to cry, I was angry, I was frustrated, and I was helpless to assist. I pulled out a business card that had my phone number on it, and I found myself saying the infamous phrase again, mostly because I didn't know what else to say.

"Steph, take this. If there is anything I can help with, let me know." It wasn't an empty offer or token of sympathy, but regardless it was too vague.

"Thank you," she said.

"I hope things work out," I said.

"Me too," she replied.

She exited the vehicle. My heart was breaking as I pulled away from the awful sight. Instantly I got a call to pick up another passenger. I wasn't sure I could get myself back into the spirt of picking people up. For those who know me, being positive is what I am good at; in that moment, I was struggling.

Then I got the notification. Steph had left me a five-star review, tipped me twenty dollars, and written a note:

'You are an exceptional driver and person. Everyone has struggles, may this little bit help you overcome a struggle.'

I had a hard time reconciling that someone in such circumstances would give the last few dollars they probably had to me when they were in such desperate need themselves. It was true, in that moment, that I didn't think I had the financial leeway to reject the funds. So it did help me overcome a struggle.

One of the things I took away from this was that, moving forward, I would never leave it as 'let me know what I can do to help.' I would always, always, offer at least two or three courses of action as options. Even close friends don't know what I can or can't do to help.

I will never forget Steph, and I hope every day that she and her brother are doing well.

I debated on adding this story into this collection. Of the nearly two thousand rides, I have so many stories I can share, but none like this. This ride left a lasting impression on my heart, and I often find myself praying for this rider.

Winter Solstice

Long dark nights rule the night sky,
everyone more than ready for the last year to say goodbye.
Bright colorful lights adorn roofs of homes and businesses,
family and friends are visiting from all distances.

The Utah powder keeps the resorts busy,
while holiday shoppers seem to always be in a tizzy.
Rideshare drivers bravely charge into the nights,
no matter the road condition, traffic, or road rage dogfights.

They rapidly take people to and fro,
carrying their most precious cargo.
Daring the weather to bring the snow,
treating destinations like islands in an archipelago.

Keeping people safe both day and night,
mostly guided by the GPS and moonlight.
To drivers be safe out there, and best wishes for many a big fare.

To passengers thank you for choosing rideshare,
you working with us is a Christmas gift.

The Airport

I join the end of the que waiting at the airport,
eager to be someone's transport.
I watch the many flights roll in,
knowing that all those waiting will eventually win.

The number of drivers slowly counts down,
hoping for a passenger who needs to go further than just into
    town.
Streams of assigned drivers pass by my car,
comforted by the fact that the terminals are not that far.

Finally, my app comes to life,
pairing me with a passenger who is in transportational strife.
Putting the vehicle in gear, I head for the terminal,
my turn to drive past those waiting to be purposeful.

I carefully navigate the never-ending construction,
watching close for people being oblivious obstructions.
Passing through the near-nonsensical speed limit zone,
I dodge the ever-changing configuration of orange cones.

Finally, I reach the first real building,
again, avoiding the non-rideshare drivers who ignorantly ignore
    the living.
I reach the designated Rideshare and Uber pickup place,
A timer is set by the airport traffic cops' grace.

I leap from my vehicle ready to assist,
making sure none of my passengers' luggage is missed.
Time counting down like a NASCAR pit crew,
I manage to get moving with seconds left in few.

Knowing that I have only fought half the battle,
I move forward to exit, herded like cattle.
I dodge anxious and excited cars leaving with much too haste;
I cautiously set a slow steady pace.

Finally, free of the dense airport gravity,
I get my passenger to their destination without casualty.
The airport can test the nerves and patients of veteran drivers,
but it is all worth it to take home all the wonderful flyers.

Slow Days

I sit eager and ready to take on a Rideshare day,
fueled, vacuumed, washed, a guest water in tray.
Parked at a very prominent crossroad,
Patiently I wait for a call with Rideshare in driver mode.

Seconds and minutes slowly tick by,
I look around and try to think of what else to try.
I look at the passenger app to see all the drivers in the area;
plethora of cars on map drives thinking into hysteria.

Worries of how to make today successful,
Thoughts on if I should stay or go I wrestle.
Drive to the molasses moving airport que,
Or drive into the downtown traffic zoo?

I look at the clock and notice an hour gone past,
With a deep sigh I consider a relent,
Head home, app turned off with some resent.
Just as my hand reaches for the phone,

I hear the long-awaited ride request tone.
I roll my eyes but quick accept,
Put the vehicle in drive heading for passenger intercept.
As I go I can only wonder,
If the rest of the day be this kind of blunder.

No one likes a slow Rideshare driving day,
Because in the end we all need the pay.

Back to Driving Rideshare

Here I am finally back driving Rideshare,
On the road once again on a late-night shift.

My temporary break partly by personal choice,
But also, partly due to a broken vehicle's rumbly voice.

Eager to once again take to the Utah roads,
And further update my chronicled Rideshare episode.

Nothing makes me happier than the knowledge,
Than breaking my family out of being to financial debt hostage.

I am grateful for all of the drivers who have come before,
Who blazed the road that I am so free to explore.

The world now knows my Rideshare story continues on,
With plans of a driving marathon.

I hope to see you all out there on the road,
With all the luck and fortune that you are owed.

Waiting

Gazing out the windshield during a rideshare gap,
Eagerly I wait to be summoned through the glow of the app.
Time ever so slowly crawls along,
the only cozy sound is that of birdsong.

Windows down, the vehicle rests in champagne slumber,
a lion ready for the next opportunity to find a newcomer.
Listening to the audiobook about the study of the humble
    bumblebee,
pausing a moment to capture a picture of trees' snow-covered
    filigree.

Seconds trudge forward with grade school anticipation,
I ponder on deep, complex, and clever word combination.
Random shaped clouds slowly drift by with pure unadulterated
    agony,
I stew on taking a break to grab some sanity.

The world nearly at a complete and utter standstill,
my thoughts begging to arrest on rotating treadmill.
A feeling of hopelessness starts to toss doubt on inaction,
and I start to review my day to consider any possible traffic
    infraction.

Rethinking my decision to stay in this spot and wait,
I start the car with intent for this spot to abdicate.
Then the most wonderfully anticipated sound fills the air,
the app chime penetrates the ears, beckoning me onto the
    thoroughfare.

Rideshare Tidbits

I wanted to share some final, thoughtful tidbits that I found while driving. These are thoughts shared with me, and thoughts that I had from experiences offering unexpected insights. It is remarkable how much is obvious once you have had a chance to really ponder certain topics that, on the surface, appear so much more complicated.

Sally the Social Psychologist

Sally was a pickup from the Salt Lake Airport, destination: Park City. Along the way, we talked about what she does. She offered this piece of knowledge.

~*~

"In society, we are taught to present ourselves with a negative narrative, to always think that we are not good enough, that our efforts, ability, and talents fall short of everyone around us. We carry this thinking into our work and home life. It is always with us, and speaks up every time we do anything—especially when we take a chance at something outside the norm.

"To change this isn't simply a matter of thinking positive, ignoring critics, or writing a gratitude journal. Just trying to think positive isn't changing the narrative; we never truly ignore critics; and we can only be grateful for the air we breathe so many times before it loses its effect. To change, I mean really change your narrative to yourself, takes active and engaged activities.

"I recommend starting with writing down your most painful memory, one that contains a failure or a regret. Just a single event. Sit down and physically write this event down on a piece of paper and include your thoughts and feelings. Then do this for ten days in a row for the same event. Then move to the next memory, and repeat the process.

"This is the very first step in the process of changing your narrative, because you are going to start seeing, realizing, and, for the first time, really analyzing the facets that make up your narrative. Then start writing down your greatest achievements and accomplishments, following the same pattern: one event, every day for ten days. Doing this, you will be able to rewrite your narrative to be a positive one."

~*~

She continued, saying that there are more steps and things that people can do, but then added that offering that would mean she would have to start charging me for the rideshare ride.

Political Science Major turned Economic Major: Melissa

I picked up a student from student housing; on my way to drop her off at a restaurant on State Street, she offered this little tidbit:

~*~

"Having been a political science major, I have a very interesting view of the economics of politicians and governments local, national, and international. Politicians seldom have the training or study to come into office with a fully flushed-out economic plan in hand. They trust advisors and experts to give them the cliff notes on the policy they are looking to put forward.

"Each policy put forward that says it will succeed is absolutely right, but at the same time is absolutely wrong. This is because there are so many variables that must be guessed to prove the policy right or wrong. So, the politicians are presented with a plan with the utmost confidence in its success, just as political opponents are told with the same utmost confidence that the plan is doomed for failure.

"So at the end of the day, who is right and who is wrong, the answer is both are both. Only time, which is a variable, will tell who was right, at least within that measurement of time. Some plans will start but will never reach full fruition to see if it would work or not; while others bloom or die quickly of success."

Thoughts on Pondering

While I waited at the airport in que for a ride, I often had time to reflect. During the summer, I would watch as the sun faded behind the horizon, and during the winter I would watch the blinking lights of incoming planes lining up to land. On a clear night, I can see about a dozen flights coming in.

I wondered about such things as if I had made the right choice in coming to the airport as opposed to waiting in the city, as opposed to hanging out in the suburbs. Every once in a while, I created a Facebook Live video, or wrote up clever little poems or thoughts to post online (which was the start of this project).

It wasn't until my second month of driving for Rideshare and waiting at the airport dozens of times, that I realized I was doing something that few people dedicate time to do. That is: meditate, thing, and ponder things. I eventually listened to a TED Talk where the speaker mentioned how important it is for our health to set aside time for ourselves.

After putting real thought into it, I also realized I was coming up with better ideas for my work. I was becoming more patient with the world, too. My everyday anxiety was dissolving into well-thought plans and purposeful direction.

So. Whether you drive rideshare or not, I highly recommend setting aside time for reflection.

The Ghost that Haunts Me

There is one city in Utah that I have incredibly strong feelings about. I had spent a lot of time in that city, at a point in life where everything seemed perfect. Then, just as fast as you can imagine, the whole world was tipped on its head. The results were devastating and soul-crushing. As a rideshare driver, I got cold chills every time I neared that particular city; every call to pick someone up from there filled me with dread. The memories there are too contradictory: the amazing meshes with the awful. I avoid it every chance I can.

There were times driving rideshare required me to go there. The hardest were the calls for passengers at the epicenter of the city, where the pain runs the deepest. Whenever I left the city again, especially without a passenger, I was deeply relieved. I looked forward to driving everywhere, anywhere, else.

I expect that someday, these feelings will soften; but I doubt they will fade completely. I know that everyone has their own ghosts that haunt them. One of mine happens to be an entire city.

Real Conversation

Over the years, I have experienced several times the pleasure and opportunity of contrary opinions at depth. These were personal conversations with individuals who didn't agree with me on a personal, fundamental, spiritual, or psychological level. They never developed into arguments; we remained always civil, and allowed each other to finish our thoughts. Driving rideshare greatly increased the number and frequency of these conversations. It has given me a deep appreciation of how amazing people are—of how they are both infinitely complex and closely relatable. Rideshare has reaffirmed my faith in humanity in general. Though as a whole we are not always the smartest, there is a glimmer of genius in everyone.

Paying Attention?

Driving away from a popular location, once, the traffic was moderate. I heard the familiar sound of a fire truck's siren. A quick check of the mirrors found that it was coming from behind me, just a little way off. I promptly turned on my turn signal and pulled to the side of the road. The road offered very little in the way of a pull off, and so half my vehicle remained in the lane.

Immediately behind me had been a large Ford pickup. I glanced in my mirror to see the white truck mash its breaks. The driver threw up their hands in irritation. With an angry face, the driver swerved their vehicle back into traffic and proceeded to flash me an offensive gesture.

That is when the irritated fire truck had to slam its breaks and honk its horn several extra times.

The driver of the white truck, clearly embarrassed at their mistake, pulled over in front of me to allow the fire truck to pass.

Is it too much to ask that people pay attention just a little more?

UDOT

I was on one of my routine runs through the airport at about 8PM on a Sunday night. It was the tail end of the airport rush, and I had already snagged two quick trips from the airport into Salt Lake to hotels. The app showed that there were about twenty-five drivers in que to pick up passengers. I had just entered the zone to be on the que as well when I got a prompt to pick up a passenger from the Delta side of the airport. As usual on a Sunday night, there was tons of traffic; and with construction complicating things, it was going to be a minute before I would arrive.

I found myself in a situation where everyone was double parked trying to pick up passengers in the rideshare zone. I changed the app to 'arrived,' and waited for a vehicle to pull out so I could grab a spot at the curb. I was startled by a knock on my passenger window. I promptly rolled it down.

"Jared?" the passenger asked.

"John?" I asked.

He nodded his head in confirmation. I put the Journey in park and clicked on the hazards. I checked traffic carefully, then jumped out to open the trunk. As with many passengers, John had attempted to open the trunk himself but was unable to find the offset handle. Even I struggle with it sometimes, and I use it all the time.

I loaded the luggage into the vehicle and closed the trunk. I noticed that he was wearing nicer jeans, a flannel shirt, and wore tan Timberland boots. John climbed into the back seat. I jumped into the driver's seat.

For a moment, I felt like a fighter pilot. I put the vehicle in drive, and clicked off the hazards. I navigated between two larger SUV's and several smaller cars that were squeezing through. As we cycled out of the airport, I managed to escape the worst of the traffic.

"John, how are you doing today?" I asked.

"Oh." He looked up from his phone. "Sorry, what?"

"How are you doing today?" I asked again.

"Ah, good, yeah, couldn't be better," he said.

As we neared the interchange, I could see that the map wanted us to take a roundabout approach. It was significantly out of the way.

"This is odd; it wants us to take 201 and down 5600," I said. I thought it would be better to mention it now to prevent confusion. The I–15 south, or even Bangerder highway, would be the commonsense routes.

"That is weird," he said. "Just take I–15."

"Sounds good," I said.

I noticed that he focused on his phone again, and after a short while he made a call. As soon as we reached the point where

I–80 connects with I–15, we were at a complete standstill. We were past the ability to change lanes or exit anywhere; we would have to wait. I could see stopped taillights for miles.

"Crazy," I said to myself.

"Dang, must be a traffic accident up ahead," John said.

"Probably," I added.

John immediately went back to working on his phone. Slowly and carefully, we inched forward.

Finally, we arrived at the choke point 45 min later. We could see traffic being funneled into one lane. I was super curious to see how bad the accident was that they had closed down six lanes. Once we were in the single lane, traffic was moving quickly. I kept looking for the accident. I drove for quite a ways before we saw three pickup trucks with flashing lights.

"Crazy, no accident," I said.

"Really?!" John asked. He finally looked up from his phone and saw the three vehicles.

"Must be a big project." I left the comment hanging with sarcasm.

"Ah, that is why it recommended 5600," he said, stating the obvious. "There is another one of these down a way, and Bangerder has them all over."

I wondered if he had read the changes online or in a newspaper. I was curious as to why and how he knew that.

"Wow, I am impressed with your road construction knowledge," I said, in an attempted ruse to get him to provide information.

He hesitated a moment before divulging, "Yeah, I am a supervisor with UDOT. I was at a conference on civilian traffic flow theory."

"Were you with them during the 2002 winter Olympics construction?" I asked.

I suspected he had heard all about the legendary construction that retrofitted the roads for the Olympics. When I first moved to Utah in 2001, UDOT was working at a feverish pace to update the highway and freeway systems. It had created what many would call "the slalom." This was because of its back and forth weaving and narrow lanes. Ever since this aggressive method was used to update the road, UDOT seems to have adopted the practice as a permanent feature. For the record, it is very painful.

"No, I wasn't on the team at that point," he said. "It was a marvel what they managed to do in the time they had, but when I came on we were still fixing things from that."

"I am curious: does everyone you know blame you for road construction?" I asked.

"They ask me about everything, especially local municipality projects," he replied.

"Fun," I added.

"Right?!" He let out a laugh.

"Do people give you credit for the improvements after they are completed?" I asked. I suspected that I knew the answer, but I had to ask.

"Every once in a while, and I mean a blue moon," John replied.

"Go figure." I offered a big grin as a follow up.

"How long have you been driving rideshare?" he asked.

"For a while now." I wasn't quite sure why I didn't tell him it had been nearly two years, but then I asked, "Why did you decide to work for UDOT?"

There was a long pause and I could see that John was deep in thought. Questions about career were typically softball questions. He leaned back and let out a deep sigh. I wasn't quite sure if I had offended him, or if maybe he had not heard me. I shot a glance at the rearview mirror. He just offered a thinking face.

"You know…" He finally offered, "that is a great question. As it turns out, it is long and complicated."

I nodded my head thoughtfully. He went silent again, then started working on his phone. As we neared the drop off point he made a call.

"Yeah," he said, "look, I know I am super late; I was stuck in traffic."

There was a long pause and a deep sigh before he continued.

"Yeah. Yeah. It was construction on I–15 that I forgot about." The sound in his voice dropped. "I am sorry, I know, me of all people. Look, can we talk about this when I get there?"

These are the moments where I try not to eavesdrop, but sometimes I can't help but hear what is going on. I turned the corner and there was construction on the street that the map had not taken into account.

"Ugh, are you kidding me?" John said. "I didn't know there was construction on the street also; I will be there in like five min."

I shook my head at the situation and proceeded to adjust the route. Sure enough, after just a few minutes we pulled up to the house that had balloons and a banner in the yard.

"Glad I could get you home," I said. "Enjoy the party."

"Yeah, thanks for the ride," he said.

I got out and opened the door for him. As he approached the house, I could hear someone asking about his late arrival. I reset the seat and headed off to the next call.

This really highlighted my complicated relationship with UDOT. Their speed and attention to detail when they have expanded certain projects, on I–15 and other state roads, had made my life as a rideshare driver and everyday commuter so much better. On the other hand, the random longevity or lane closures has time and again complicated and frustrated. I couldn't help but relish the trip that was dripping with pure irony.

Jovial and Jointing

One of my many lives is being a Rideshare driver,
loving the job over that of using a screwdriver or pliers to earn an
extra ten spot or fiver.

I thrived on the thrilling conversation,
with doctors, lawyers, engineers, scientists, scholars, students, silly
and sober while taking them to their destinations.

I would pick their brains to understand their thought trains,
questions of who, what, when, why and even how accurate those
gene tests are from ancestry and other thought plains.

I would travel back and forth, to and fro,
many times, from airport to Park City and even once from airport
to Logan trying to avoid driving in the snow.

Though I took up the job because I enjoyed it,
the truth is I did it out of necessity, supporting family and to pay
the bills and bit.

So off in the Dodge Journey I drove into the night,
running around bringing joy to people of all types, shapes, and
height.

Loving the experience and the good time,
I recommend Rideshare so much I wrote this little rhyme.

Car Accident

Now having driven for Rideshare for several months,
I feel as though I have been through my lumps.
Though I have seen every kind of passenger true,
there is one thing I have seen that makes me blue.

I have seen most types and shapes of vehicle,
with scratches, dents, missing windshields, missing all things
    feasible.
Cars, Vans, Trucks, SUV tumbled,
their metal skeletons twisted and crumbled.

Fire trucks and ambulances over scattered debris,
officers secure the accident site and surrounding typography.
Family lives instantly torn apart,
tragically sometimes stealing the life from someone's unfortunate
    heart.

So many reasons that cause the collisions,
mostly due to one person's poor decisions.
I hate that thing that haunts most everyone,
I wish I had the power to make accidents undone.

Take great care while driving out there,
it will happen to the poor and the millionaire.
Let's all get home safe at the end of the night,
remember in an accident it doesn't matter who was right.

In Conclusion

My rideshare career was cut short by the 2020 Covid-19 outbreak. I had actively driven in Park City during the 2020 Sundance Film Festival, which many speculate was a key super spreader event for the virus. There were roughly 120,000 people crammed into small theaters, restaurants, and hotels. (This could only be speculation, as the Wuhan lockdown started on January 23rd, the same day the film festival started. Little was known at that moment and testing was uncommon or non-existent.)

It was after Sundance that Lisa and I starting have hard conversations about our finances, and balancing them against risk. Jack did not have his new heart yet and had a compromised immune system. We were well short of our goals. With no confirmed cases of Covid-19 in Utah, we decided to proceed with caution. I would try to avoid the airport because we thought that would be the greatest risk.

My last ride was March 6th, 2020. I remember my last passenger very well. He was going to a bar in downtown Salt Lake, and we talked about Covid-19. My passenger was already under

244 § Jared Quan

the influence when I picked him up, and he droned on about conspiracies that the Pentaverate was behind the made-up illness.

For those who don't know, the Pentaverate is a comedic conspiracy that Mike Myers brings to life in the 1993 "So I Married an Axe Murder" movie. Mike Myers' character, Stuart Mackenzie, claims that "the Queen, the Vatican, the Gettys, the Rothschilds, and Colonel Sanders before he went tits-up" made up the secret organization. (This was before the Mike Myers "Pentaverate" series on Netflix.)

When I returned home on March 6th, I discovered that Utah had its first confirmed COVID-19 case, an elderly 60-year-old man who had been on a cruise. Utah Governor Herbert issued a state of emergency. The task forces were already at work tracing and confirming quarantine.

It was that night that we decided to hold off driving rideshare until things became clearer. The next day, March 7th, I volunteered at the Salt Lake City Downtown Library for the Utah Film Center with two of my daughters. The library was busy, and the event was well-attended. With the news of the Utah case, the Utah Film Center added sanitizer and disinfected often. It was at the event that the Utah Film Center wisely suspended the rest of the event for the remaining days it was scheduled.

March 11th is when everything shifted. That is when Rudy Gobert, center for the Utah Jazz basketball team, jokingly touched all of the reporter's microphones. Then he tested positive for

Covid-19. As soon as the NBA shut down its games, everyone took notice. Just a few weeks later my company sent everyone to work from home.

After talking things through with the transplant team, Lisa and I decided to suspend driving until after the pandemic was over. I messaged the primary Rideshare company that I drove for and let them know that I was going to suspend driving, due to the outbreak and my son's condition. They responded by letting me know that they had suspended my account until I could prove that I didn't have Covid-19 with a negative test.

I was a little disappointed at their response, after three years' employment and an overall five-star (4.94) rating with one thousand nine hundred and forty-seven rides. I was tired, my vehicles were worn, and the company I had fallen in love with driving rideshare for broke up with me via a cold email. With that response, I was ready to retire from driving rideshare wholesale.

As I mentioned at the beginning of the book, Jack got his heart late 2020. What I didn't mention was during his recovery, I came down with COVID-19. Despite quarantining, my family came down with it as well. Thankfully, Jack was still safe in the hospital while we went through that particular adventure, which eventually sent Lisa to the hospital too. Once the whole family recovered, we were able to bring Jack home, three weeks after he was initially cleared to leave.

Despite my best efforts and my side gigs, I came up well short of the goal we needed to take care of Jack's medicines. The community rallied to come to our aid. I will never forget the amazing miracles that helped us through the end. As of the completion of this book, Jack is doing well.

I ended up adopting a far less lucrative, but fun, way to take up the time I once spent driving rideshare. I started streaming on Twitch and went on to become an affiliate. Thanks to that, I still make some money, and am excited to see what happens next.

I will never forget the thousands of adventures I went on. I have so many stories left to tell, but wanted to share some of my personal favorites in this book. I hope you enjoyed this! I thank you so much for purchasing this, as every bit helps with the lifetime of medications Jack requires for his new heart.

Really Random and Ridiculous Rideshare Rumors

Wind rushing below my feet armed with newly formed treads,
while most people lay sleeping in their beds.
Eagerly I offer my driving skill with vagabond neurosis,
All while keeping things carefully within ketosis.

Having completed over a thousand crusades, campaigns and
      sorties,
as chauffeur, therapist, concierge, footman, advocate, dealing with
      the kind and warty.
With rain forest skill, I absorb and store everything,
as whispers, rumors, thoughts, ideas, and all manner of air
      through lips sing.

Always with terminuses common and surprisingly ultra-rare,
From airport to hotel, apartment, or multi-million-dollar homes
      beyond compare.
Mingling with the privileged to the emotionally downtrodden,
Regardless of status, class or rank, each my horizons did broaden.

Real life is much, much stranger than fiction,
It's hard to give full breath in this modest depiction.
I have heard the most interesting things,
Here are a few for your understandings:

I once picked up a trio from a concert venue, who were all three
      fairly intoxicated,
bragging how they teach at the college after drinking tons of
      alcohol feeling unappreciated.
Two friends of Senegalese descent whispered of a fast-food boss
      who's narcoleptic on the clock,

they had caught him sleeping anywhere he could lean and worried
    he might start to sleepwalk.

A geneticist told me that Crisper won't take us to Gattaca,
it will take us to the brink, stopping short of human designer
    Anastatica.
One microbiologist said that an over-the-counter medicine kills
    people every day,
but no one mentions its name when its harm is done to everyone's
    dismay.

Whisperings of a federal Grant Writer mentioned there is money
    set aside for most anything,
deep sea exploration, studies on cohabitation, performance on
    stage and writers for wellspring.
Two Air Force Pilots looking remarkably like Zac Efron chatted
    about how they were excited,
for new technology and wished it was expedited.

Former Major League Baseball Player and wife bragged about
    their sports-driven offspring,
mentioned a celebrated MLB pitcher couldn't hit the side of a
    barn in college with his best sling.
An emergency medical technician who spends most of his time
    flying to remote places,
Remarked that he has seen more than lights in the sky suggesting
    alien races.

A humble young culinary student, working hard towards their
    degree to be a chef,
wanted to share with the world their thoughts on government
    conspiracy to make people deaf.
A banker from Bosnia talked on and on about how she missed the
    European cities,

she slipped in her thought that the world is flat and there should
     be a congressional committee.

Once an airline pilot said to me that in his thirty-five years of
     flying he had seen so much,
Crazy people ranting, medical emergencies, went on about visions
     he was having and such.
One person I picked up from a bar who was inebriated,
mumbled about ghosts, then he exited as if he evaporated.

A nice psychic headed to the airport, let me know how much she
     loved the rideshare people,
She let me know that the world isn't what it seems, and that
     everything is actually sepal.
There are too many stories to tell in one sitting, with abductions
     by government or alien alike,
Things heard so unbelievable would almost be dismissed if
     something about it didn't strike.
If you want to hear the greatest variety of things,
Try rideshare driving, and imagination won't need any wellsprings.

About The Author
Jared Quan

Silver Quill Award Winner

Olive Woolley Burt First Honorable Mention

Jared is an Author/Gamer/Writer—Twitch Affiliate, a former writer for SI.com and Yahoo. Published works include Changing Wax, Ezekiel's Gun, and Really Random and Ridiculous Ride-share Rumors. He has served in key roles with Storymakers, League of Utah Writers, Cultural Arts Society of West Jordan, EMAA, Big World Network, TEDxSaltLakeCity, UVU Book Academy, Utah Poet Laureate Selection Committee, and countless events/organizations. Jared has received awards from two Presidents of the United States, from Utah State Governor, Lt. Governor, and recognition from many other organizations. He has been interviewed by several websites and podcasts, including Joseph Batzel, Artifice, and Writing Excuses Podcast.

Website: JaredQuan.com

Bibliography

[i] Ward, Adrian F. "The Neuroscience of Everybody's Favorite Topic." Scientific American, Scientific American, 16 July 2013, https://www.scientificamerican.com/article/the-neuroscience-of-everybody-favorite-topic-themselves/.

[ii] Lambert, Craig. "Choosing Confidants." Harvard Magazine, Harvard Magazine, January-February 2015, https://www.harvardmagazine.com/2015/01/choosing-confidants

www.ingramcontent.com/pod-product-compliance
Lightning Source LLC
LaVergne TN
LVHW051227080426
835513LV00016B/1453